T0208508

Paroxysm

Paroxysm

Interviews with Philippe Petit

◆

Jean Baudrillard

Translated by Chris Turner

VERSO
London • New York

First published by Verso 1998
This edition © Verso 1998
Translation © Chris Turner 1998
First published as *Le Paroxyste indifférent: Entretiens avec Philippe Petit*
© Editions Grasset & Fasquelle 1997
All rights reserved

Verso
UK: 6 Meard Street, London W1V 3HR

US: 180 Varick Street, New York, NY 10014–4606

Verso is the imprint of New Left Books

ISBN 978-1-85984-241-6

British Library Cataloguing in Publication Data
A catalogue record for this book is available from the British Library

Library of Congress Cataloging-in-Publication Data
Baudrillard, Jean.
[Paroxyste indifférent. English]
Paroxysm: interviews with Philippe Petit / Jean Baudrillard:
translated by Chris Turner.
p.   cm.
ISBN 1–85984–241–0 (paper). — ISBN 1–85984–844–3 (cloth)
1. Baudrillard, Jean—Interviews. 2. Sociologists—France—
Interviews. 3. Postmodernism. I. Petit, Philippe. 1951–
II. Title.
HM22.F8B3813 1998   98–39610
301—dc21   CIP

Typeset by M Rules
Printed and bound by
The Bath Press

In prosody, the term 'paroxytone', the literal equivalent of which in Latin is the penultimate, refers to the syllable before last. The paroxysm might thus be said to be the penultimate moment, that is to say not the final moment, but the moment just before the end, just before there's nothing more to be said.

Contents

The Destiny of Value

The end of political economy is a thing we dreamt of with Marx. It was a dream in which classes died out and the social sphere became transparent, according to an ineluctable logic of the crisis of capital. Then we dreamed the dream against Marx himself, disavowing the postulates of economics. A radical alternative, this, denying any primacy to the economic or political spheres in first or last instance: political economy quite simply abolished as epiphenomenon, vanquished by its own simulacrum and by a higher logic. We no longer even need to dream of that end today. Political economy is disappearing by its own hand before our very eyes; it is turning into a trans-economics of speculation and flouting its own logic (the law of value, of the market, production, surplus-value, the very logic of capital), as it develops into a game with floating, arbitrary rules, a *jeu de catastrophe*. Political economy will have come to an end, but not at all as we expected it to – it will have ended by becoming exacerbated to the point of parody. Speculation is no longer surplus-value; it is the ecstasy of value, without reference to production or its real conditions. It is the pure and empty form, the expurgated form of value, which plays now on its own orbital circulation and revolution alone. It is by destabilizing itself monstrously – ironically, as it were – that political economy short-circuits every alternative. For what can you do against such a constant upping of the stakes, which, in its own way, takes over the energy of potlatch, of poker, of the challenge to its own logic, and represents, as it were, the transition to the aesthetic and frenzied phase of the economy – a way of putting an end to the economy that is the most singular in style, ultimately more original than our political utopias? Faced with this dangerous leap, can theory make a double leap to maintain its advantage?

The great Nietzschean idea of the transvaluation of all values has seen itself realized in precisely the opposite way: in the involution of all values. We have not passed beyond, but fallen short of Good and Evil, short of the True and the False, short of the Beautiful and the Ugly – we have passed not into a dimension that is the product of excess, but into one generated by lack. There has been neither transmutation nor surpassing, but dissolution and loss of distinction.

We dreamt of a transgressive, excessive mutation of values. What is coming about is a regressive, recessive, involutive mutation. *Diesseits von Gut und Böse. Requiescat* Nietzsche.

For the transmutation of values we substituted the commutation of values, for their reciprocal transfiguration we substituted their indifference one to another and their confusion. Their transdevaluation, so to speak. The contemporary conjuncture, in which all values are rehabilitated and indiscriminately permutated, is the worst there has been. Even the distinction between the useful and the useless can no longer be made, given the excess of functionality which entails their contamination – this is the death knell of use-value. The true cancels itself in the truer-than-true, the too-true-to-be-true – the reign of simulation. The false disappears into the too-false-to-be-false – the end of the aesthetic illusion. And the loss of evil is even more painful than the loss of good, the loss of the false even more painful than the loss of the true.

We are attempting to rehabilitate all these values today, one by one, but what we do not know how to re-create is the electricity generated by their contradiction. It is the same with individual values: we have rehabilitated them not in their dialectical tension with the social, but on the same basis as the social – as endangered masterpieces.

Emptied of this negative tension, they become equivalent, substitutable. Each shows through in the other – good shows through in evil, the false in the true, the ugly in the beautiful, the masculine in the feminine, and vice versa. Each one squints out through the other. A generalized strabismus of value. We are a long way from a tension between, or a collision of, values, such as equates with an upsurge of energy, in the way the collision between matter and antimatter would equate with a definitive release of energy. When the false takes over all the energy of the true – or vice versa – then art is produced, or illusion. When the real absorbs all the energy of the unreal, fiction results. On the other hand, when the true loses even its opposite energy, that of the imaginary, the outcome is simulation, the lowest degree of illusion. When the good loses even the energy of evil, the lowest degree of morality ensues.

It is the same with all systems, including value systems, which are characterized by losing their reference points and passing beyond their ends. Once beyond their initial determinations and their own principles, they become metastatic, in the literal sense of any biological process radiating out into the whole body. Thus sex is no longer in sex, the political no longer in the political. They are anywhere but. The aesthetic itself is like a filterable virus. All categories give way to a kind of hypersyncretism, homeostasis and indistinction.

But is this kind of unrestrained superfusion, irradiation, virality of value – at the end of which it invests, or rather infects, everything with an irresistible epidemic process – the product of a move beyond value or, by contrast, the sign of an impossibility of denying itself as such? As for being beyond value, we are certainly that – what with the flows of money on the stock exchange and capital running wild, to speak only of the economy. But is this the achieved utopia of value? It seems rather that value has itself also chosen a fatal strategy, that it has chosen to pass beyond its own ends by a total release of its energy into the void, by liquidating everything and charging on regardless.

All that can be set against the destiny of value is the destiny of form. All forms have successively dissipated into values, just as the various forms of energy dissipate into heat. Dissipating into aesthetics as value, into morality as value, into ideology as value. But values themselves dissipate and, by a process of perpetual acceleration similar to the Brownian motion of molecules, end up being confused, as indifferent and equivalent, within a fractal, random, statistical universe. In this way we lost use-value, then good old exchange-value, obliterated by speculation, and we are currently losing even sign-value for an indefinite signaletics, losing any differential logic of the sign for an undifferentiated circulation of machine logics. And even the sign is not what it was. Physical entropy, metaphysical entropy: every value stands under the sign of entropy, and every difference under the sign of indifference. All that lives by difference will perish by indifference. All that lives by value will perish by equivalence. All that lives by meaning will perish by insignificance. And it is because we no longer know what is true or false, what is good or evil, what has value or does not, that we are forced to store everything, record everything, conserve everything, and from this an irrevocable devaluation ensues. Is it because there is no longer any criterion of value that we accumulate things infinitely, or is it because we have set about storing, accumulating, adding reality to reality and information to information that all values have become confused and undecidable? Even this is undecidable.

Against the differential play of value, the dual play of form: reversibility and metamorphosis. Forms do not differ between themselves: they are all singular and incomparable. And it is because they are incomparable that we experience them, like language, as a happy catastrophe – or as the incomparable duality of the masculine and the feminine, which exist only to seduce one another, without ever being reconciled. Neither active nor passive, neither subject nor object, neither singular nor plural: such is the dual and reversible mode which, from one form to the other, maintains a radical distance and a secret connivance – a predestined progression.

Metamorphosis itself is a happy catastrophe: it is the ceaseless changing of the one sex into the other, of ideas one into the other, of tones, words and colours. It is the changing of the human into the inhuman, and on through the total cycle of appearances, forms and substances respectively: vegetable, mineral, animal and human. And why not of other superhuman forms once the human is no longer the be-all and end-all?

Over against the disenchanted hypothesis of value stands the enchanted hypothesis of form. For if all values do indeed seem to be disappearing as part of an irresistible process, forms, for their part, seem indestructible – at least in dreams. And the trap we can fall into is that of wishing to save values at all costs, when the fundamental loss could be said to be the loss of forms.

4

PART ONE

Why Is There Nothing
Rather Than Something?

Chapter 1
Endgame

Philippe Petit: At the beginning of your book *The Illusion of the End* (1992/94), you give the impression of having taken leave of history once and for all. You speak of the disappearance of history, of the idea that 'history, meaning and progress are no longer able to reach their escape velocity', and that the event, as a result of being driven out of its original sphere by information and the media, no longer circulates in memories, but in computer memory banks. 'History', you also write, 'is no longer able to transcend itself . . . ; it is . . . imploding into current events.'

Doesn't a diagnosis of this kind mean that all hope of political change is condemned from the outset? How does it allow us to escape from the world of those who believe in nothing and seem fated to ruminate on that nothing? Has history taken its leave of you, or is this you signing its death certificate?

Jean Baudrillard: Neither of those things. In that chapter, which I called 'Pataphysics of the Year 2000', I set out from the idea that we shall not get back to history as it was before information and the media, that the excess of history or the excess of eventfulness cancelled out the very possibility of historical action. It isn't that there are more events, but the event in itself is multiplied by its dissemination, by news and information. I'd say that it's because everything has become history that it's no longer possible to believe in history. Mentalities, daily life, sexuality –

everything has been historicalized. It is, then, rather by excess than by rarefaction that we have gradually lost the concept and meaning of history. This is not the end of history in Fukuyama's sense, by the resolution of all the contradictions to which it had given rise, but the dilution of history as event: its media *mise en scène*, its excess of visibility. The continuity of time, which is a way of defining history (for there to be a possible recurrence of a sequence of meaning there has necessarily to be a past, a present and a future, with a continuity between them), is less and less certain. With instant information, there's no longer any time for history itself. In a sense, it doesn't have time to take place. It's short-circuited. To point this out isn't to believe in nothing any more, as you put it, but to register this curving back of history and try to thwart its lethal effects.

PP: Why put so much stress, then, on the idea that 'imagining the future is beyond us'? This suggests that we must always expect the worst. And then the fall of communism was no small event! European history well and truly awoke from its dogmatic slumbers. Even if the landscape after the battle in the Balkans is, to say the least, damaged. . . .

JB: With the end of communism, we told ourselves: 'History is beginning again'. This is a form of the incantation or hallucination of a new perspective. The history of Central and Eastern Europe had been frozen and, once unfrozen, it took on a new look. It isn't the reappearance of a history in progress, with a future in its kit-bag, that has emerged. It's the revival of a history that has already taken place. It's a phantom history that's coming back to haunt the post-communist societies. 'A reverse rewriting of the whole twentieth century.' A collage of the residues of history. In the homeostatic space of the new world order, the two systems are exchanging their residues by a perverse contamination. Unfrozen liberty in the East and magnified, museified liberty in the West are the two sides of a single coin. And the parallel events, such as nationalism, which we see re-emerging, no longer have the same meaning in a history in the making and a history being unmade, in an ascending history or a repentant history.

PP: They no longer have the same meaning, but they do have meaning, none the less. . . .

JB: Events collide and succeed one another, but they don't engender new relations of force. They are, as it were, stuck in the past, in past problems. Yesterday's problems are there, but we no longer know how to solve them and there is no means of making way for some new event. There was, admittedly, an illusion of a perspective in 1989, but we very quickly saw that the protagonists of that 'happy ending' had no more cards up their sleeve. So the recycling of history began, we began to live out the film backwards. . . .

Today we look solely to the symbolic term of the millennium to set us off again. The year 2000 as sole fatidical non-event. A magical waiting, itself millenarian, for non-parousia. In the meanwhile, everyone's lying low – creeping catalepsy, collective catatonia, eyes riveted on the countdown. But this is an empty suspense: it's as though the whole of the twentieth century were emptying itself of its substance in these few years, as though it were scaling down all its demands to the point of wiping out the very traces of its history.

PP: Perhaps. But you can't deny that communism has failed and the collapse of the Soviet system has actually occurred!

JB: The communist system and the Berlin Wall didn't fall outwards, as a mark of openness and freedom, but inwards, as a mark of disintegration and of a dismantling that was violent, but had no liberatory consequences. They self-destructed, leaving behind an empty space, as when buildings implode. The only thing that collapse released was the contagious germs of collapse. And this, in fact, is what happened with the USSR: what immediately gravitated, or radiated, out from there were ferments of deliquescence and disappearance, or of blackmail by threat of disappearance, which the East European countries have joyously exported to the West, in exchange for which they have, in the guise of freedom, earned themselves irradiation by free-market capitalism and a system of values much more efficient than their own, but one that is equally deliquescent. An exchange of courtesies in which we can see that the Wall protected the West from the East as much as the opposite. In which we can see that communism at least preserved the fiction of Western values. Which might make one hope for its rehabilitation, or its return, or something equivalent – as a last-ditch measure for re-polarizing the world.

PP: In the meantime, what is happening?

JB: The two systems are contaminating each other. The one sends the other its technologies and markets; the other sends back its pollution, viruses and angst. Things aren't finally settled, but I think what has triumphed isn't capitalism but the global, so to speak, and the price paid has been the disappearance of the universal in terms of a value system. We are, admittedly, seeing a kind of excrescence of human rights and democracy, but only in so far as their efficacy has long since disappeared. We're no longer in a power struggle between two systems, but in a kind of negative competition to see who'll be first to get their hands on their own values and sell them off – it's a liquidation race.

Communism and its marvellous, life-size collapse – that is to say, its collapse on a grand historical scale – is the liquidation of the social, of the political as idea, as value, as utopian ideal, in the disaster of achieved utopia. But isn't it the same in the West: the life-size failure of the achieved utopia of happiness? The collapse of the Western value system is precisely correlative with the collapse of communism in Eastern Europe. Western stupefaction, that of a happiness fuelled by hormones and animal feed, this flabby, technological ecstasy, this interactive virus we pass over to Eastern Europe in exchange for its opening-up to democracy, is even worse than the opposite contagion of totalitarianism, of rigid control and bureaucratic inertia. It's the corruption of the visible, as against the corruption of the hidden, the secret, the repressed. The year 1989 can be seen to have marked the beginning of the immense reciprocal contamination of the two worlds. And perhaps the deliquescence, the disintegration of the capitalist world, of its principles and values, even preceded that of socialism in the East? Perhaps this latter fell into line with the

Western world's indifference to its own values – no longer having before it any ideology, any political will worthy of the name? All that's different is today forced to capitulate before the undifferentiated universe. Entropy has won, the entropy of the market and democracy, pulling irresistibly towards a generalized exchangism of all values. Hence the wave of revisionism sweeping across a Western world conscious of this irresistible degradation, and tempted finally to restore some good old values (including that of communism) to rescue its own identity. Here we have communism at last become a humanism!

PP: What is capitalism for you today?

JB: I really don't know. It's a sort of dilution of the universal in a global state of affairs. It's a sort of purely operational general equivalent. It no longer even involves any opposing or negative values, such as revolution or the indignity of labour. For a long time the communists proposed an antagonistic system. There's no antagonistic system today simply because the system itself no longer has any values or gravity. All that remains is an automatic transcription of the world into the global.

PP: What distinction do you draw between the universal and the global?

JB: In the global, all differences fade and de-intensify, giving way to a pure and simple circulation of exchanges. All liberties fade before the mere liberation of exchange. Globalization and universality don't go together; they might be said, rather, to be mutually exclusive. Globalization is the globalization of technologies, the market, tourism, information. Universality is the universality of values, human rights, freedoms, culture, democracy. Globalization seems irreversible; the universal might be said, rather, to be on its way out. At least as it has constituted itself as a system of values on the scale of Western modernity, which is something that has no equivalent in any other culture. Even a living, contemporary culture like the Japanese has no term for it. No word to refer to a system of values which regards itself as attuned to all cultures and their difference but which, paradoxically, does not conceive itself as relative, and aspires, in all ingenuousness, to be the ideal transcendence of all the others. We don't imagine for a moment that the universal might merely be the particular style of thinking of the West, its specific product – an original one, admittedly, but in the end no more exportable than any other local product. Yet this is how the Japanese see it – as a specific, Western feature – and, far from signing up to an abstract concept, they, by a strange twist, relativize our universal and incorporate it into their singularity.

PP: Why are you so absolutely intent on the universal dissolving into the particular culture of a people? I don't mind admitting with you that rationalist moralism has had a chequered history, and that the betrayal of the universal denounced by Benda in 1927 is no longer the issue today, but I can't see why the reconstruction of the Enlightenment ideal would be such an impossible task? After Adorno, there is Habermas. . . .

JB: Every culture worthy of the name meets its ruin in the universal. Every culture which universalizes itself loses its singularity and dies away. This is how it is with those we've destroyed by their enforced assimilation, but it's also how it is with ours in its pretension to universality. The difference is that the others died of their singularity, which is a noble death, whereas we're dying from the loss of all singularity, from the extermination of all our values, which is a senseless death. We believe that the fate of every value is to be elevated to universality, without gauging the mortal danger that promotion represents: far from being an elevation, it is a reduction or, alternatively, an elevation to the degree zero of value. In Enlightenment times, universalization occurred at the top, by an upward progression. Today, it happens at the bottom, by a neutralization of values due to their proliferation and indefinite extension. This is how it is with human rights, democracy, etc.: their expansion corresponds to their weakest definition, their maximum entropy. Degree Xerox of value. It's the triumph of *la pensée unique*[1] over universal thought. What becomes globalized is, first of all, the market, the promiscuity of all exchanges and all products, the perpetual flow of money. In cultural terms, it's the promiscuity of all signs and all values – or, in other words, pornography. For the worldwide broadcasting and parading of everything and anything over the networks is pornography. There's no need for sexual obscenity; this interactive copulation suffices. At the end of this process, there's no longer any difference between the global and the universal. The universal itself is globalized: democracy, human rights, circulate precisely like any global product, like oil or capital. Given all this, we may ask ourselves whether the universal hasn't already succumbed to its own critical mass, and if it has ever had anything but lip-service paid to it, or found a place anywhere but in official moralities. At any rate, for us the mirror of the universal is broken (we can, in fact, see in this something like the mirror-stage of humanity). But perhaps this represents an opportunity, for, in the fragments of this broken mirror, all the singularities re-emerge. The ones we thought threatened survive; the ones we thought had disappeared revive. The increasingly intense resistances to globalization – social and political resistances, which may seem like an archaic rejection of modernity at all costs – have to be seen as harbouring an original defiant reaction to the sway of the universal. Something which goes beyond the economic and the political. A kind of agonizing revisionism in respect of the established positions of modernity, in respect of the idea of progress and history – a kind of rejection not only of the famous global technostructure, but of the mental structure of the identification of all cultures and all continents in the concept of the universal. This resurgence – or even insurrection – of singularity may assume violent, anomalous, irrational aspects from the viewpoint of 'enlightened' thought – it may take ethnic, religious or linguistic forms but also, at the individual level, temperamental and neurotic ones. But it would be a basic error (the very error one sees emerging in the moral orchestration of the politically correct discourse common to all the powers that be, and to many 'intellectuals') to condemn all these upsurges out of hand as populist, archaic or even terroristic. Everything which constitutes an event today is done against the universal, against that abstract universality (including the frantic antagonism of Islam to Western values – it's because it's the most vehement protest against this Western globalization that Islam is the number one enemy today). If we will not understand this, we'll be caught up in an endless and point-less wrestling match between a universal thought assured of its power and good conscience and an ever greater number of implacable singularities. Even in our societies, which are acculturated to the universal, you can see that none of what has been sacrificed to this concept has really disappeared. It has simply gone underground. And what is now running backwards is a whole self-styled pro-gressive history, a whole evolutionism crystallized on its end point – an end point which has, in fact, in the meantime been lost sight of. That utopia has fallen apart today, and its deep-level dislocation is advancing even more quickly than its con-solidation by force.

PP: That dislocated utopia is not entirely unlike Nietzsche's last man. It's a stan-dard democratic utopia reduced to its simplest expression. . . .

JB: Its congenital illusion is precisely the democratic illusion. We have before us a complex three-term arrangement: there is the globalization of exchanges, the uni-versality of values and the singularity of forms (languages, cultures, individuals and characters, but also chance, accident, etc. – all that the universal, in keeping with its law, impugns as an exception or an anomaly). Now, as universal values lose some of their authority and legitimacy, the situation changes and becomes more radical. So long as they could assert themselves as mediating values, they were (more or less well) able to integrate the singularities as differences, in a universal culture of dif-ference. They can no longer do this, however, as triumphant globalization sweeps away all differences and values, ushering in a perfectly in-different (un)culture. And once the universal has disappeared, once the universal is out of the equation, all that remains is the all-powerful global technostructure standing over against the singu-larities which have gone back to the wild state and been thrown back on their own devices.

The universal has had its historical chance. But today, confronted with a new world order to which there is no alternative, with an irrevocable globalization on the one hand and the waywardness or tenacious insurrection of singularities on the other, the concepts of liberty, democracy and human rights cut a very pale figure indeed, being merely the phantoms of a vanished universal. And it's hard to imagine that universal rising from its ashes, or to believe things can be sorted out by the mere play of politics – this latter being caught up in the same deregulation, and having barely any more substance to it than intellectual or moral power. Matters are not, however, finally settled, even if it's now all up with universal values. In the void left by the universal, the stakes have risen, and globalization isn't certain to be the winner. In the face of its homogenizing, solvent power, we can see heterogeneous forces springing up all over, forces which are not only different, but antagonistic and irreducible.

PP: Are you wholly intent on demoralizing the West?

JB: The demoralization of the West is constitutive of its history. I didn't invent it. 'The new sentimental order', the order of disaffection, repentance and the 'victim society', is the extension of a crisis of meaning which began in the nineteenth century with the fallout from the Industrial Revolution and colonization, and has continued throughout our long twentieth century. For thirty years we've been living in the last phase of it – or rather, the penultimate one – that is to say, the paroxystic phase. Other people's misery and humanitarian catastrophes have become our last stamping ground for adventurers.

What's called 'the new world order' has nothing of a historical field about it any more. It's a kind of horizontal field in which everyone must find their mark. If they don't, or won't, they will be forced to. From this point of view, the 'new world order' is a fundamentalist concept. It's the fundamentalism of the void, but all the fiercer for that. The essential fault line today runs through Islam, but it also runs through the heart of every so-called civilized, democratic country – and certainly even through each of us.

PP: Let's desert the West!

JB: At all events, we have to look to other worlds than the Western. The underdeveloped or developing societies are no longer what they were, since the very concept of development has been a damp squib. Precisely in their inability to achieve a coherent democratic (economic and political) principle, these societies are perhaps the foreshadowing of a later state of events, in which all societies, including our own, will have to confront the collapse of all these fine rational principles (but the 'advanced' societies have hardly achieved such a coherent democratic principle themselves, and what they have handed on to the rest of the world has been the failed, caricatured version of the model). This fateful situation is perhaps an opportunity, then. And in this sense, it is *those* societies, in their very confusion, which are in the van, not *our Western* societies, which are so proud of their technological lead and so full also of a fierce and *bien-pensant* evolutionism which prevents them from thinking anything but the world supremacy of their model. That supremacy is merely virtual – and today, moreover, it employs virtual technologies (now, technology, in common with every other medium, is double-edged, and the power of the virtual is a virtual power).

Furthermore, this model is itself going to the dogs; it's on its last legs, and is merely the ruin, the shadow, of itself. Or, more exactly, it could be said to be like the man who has lost his shadow, and has become transparent, irradiated by his own energy and infected at a deep level by his own viruses. Even from the standpoint of the evolutionism to which they adhere, the pole position of these societies is, then, problematic and imperilled. They are seeing the resurgence of all the singularities and anomalies they claimed to have abolished, and we can see them, like the societies of the Third World (which will also have served to prefigure our situation), breaking down economically and politically. Even the most solidly established nations are beginning to break up (Corsica, the Basque Country, Lombardy, Russia, Canada. Once the mirror of deterrence has been shattered, the end of the twofold division of the world is making way for general dissemination, for fractality). The future lies with the adolescent societies which will not have taken the route through economics and politics, but can cope very well with the technological without burdening themselves with all these – humanist and rational – historical categories; or, in other words, with values which are in any case turning round against themselves today, and revealing their impotence.

PP: When you say that 'in most current conflicts, all that is involved is a police-style "homeopathic violence" internal to the system', I find that hard to follow. How can you speak of homeopathic violence with regard to Iraq or the former Yugoslavia?

JB: With these conflicts, we're no longer in historical violence of the kind that might give birth, dialectically, to a history. What is dominant is an absolute model of order and peace – homeostatic, if you like, rather than homeopathic. We no longer wish to wage war, but we act in the name of a duty to contain all possible disorder. The Americans parachuted peace into Bosnia in exactly the same way as they parachuted war into Iraq. What we have here is a model in which peace and war are concertinaed, the two being indistinct today, as Orwell accurately foresaw. From the standpoint of this parachuting operation, whether or not there are thousands of deaths is immaterial. The Gulf operation could have been carried out without a single fatality: this was in fact the case on the American side. That was a war that was clean from the technological and conceptual points of view. But this is no longer a war. It is the same police-style violence in peace and war.

PP: Both history and war are losing their substance. 'The West is militarily impotent to react to Serbian aggression to the precise degree that it finds it impossible to risk the life of a single soldier,' you wrote in your column in *Libération* while Sarajevo was being bombed. Perhaps war has no future in Western Europe, but doesn't it still have one in Eastern Europe?

JB: Violence is a relation of otherness. Between the Pentagon and the Iraqis, the whole space was taken up by technology. There was no room for the violence of war properly so-called. In Bosnia, the violence is real, terrible, ambiguous. And it isn't just an old quarrel between *frères ennemis*. It's also, taken all in all, a form of revolt against the world order. The violence of war is not a mere resurgence of the past; it can express a sort of surge of vital energy, like hatred, against a 'cleansing' in all fields at the global level.

PP: Wouldn't it be more accurate to speak of emergence rather than resurgence?

JB: I entirely agree that we should view the war in the Balkans in its radical contemporary setting: that of globalization and the identity-based reactions it provokes. Seen that way, the exacerbation of national, linguistic and religious sentiment, or of a sense of identity, is a form of singular resistance. It doesn't arise in the name of any universal. It doesn't seek to organize itself. Singularities don't organize among themselves; they confront one another. They have no mission to discover a universal ascent of humanity. I even believe they are the product of the universal's disappearing beneath the global order. Every community fights for a kind of exceptionality and singularity. From this it makes a set of rules – and possibly a murderous, destructive one.

PP: Isn't citizenship a form of historical goal?

JB: The problem is one of knowing what might give it form. Where would the new balance be between the universal and the particular? Where would the system of representation be which is capable of giving form to an identity that respected the universal?

PP: Why do you think global time is the only time there can be?

JB: I don't know if it's the only time there can be, but I see it is coming. It's succeeded in creating a monopoly out of a balanced plurality. So these fine ideas of citizenship, which may be shared by individuals on the ground, have already been kidnapped, taken hostage. Moreover, the global system speaks a universalistic, pluralistic language very well. That's its official language, and that's what it operates behind. All the pious values of citizenship are being liquidated. To these old values and that distant utopia of the universal I prefer values which are their own justification in a kind of existential 'acting-out': 'I exist. I'm so-and-so, I exist.' That is to say, an assertion of identity, not as a desperate acknowledgement, but as a challenge.

PP: But identity isn't singularity?

JB: Indeed it isn't. These reactions are the desperate search for a mirror in which to find a self-image. Today, whether it be groups, nations or individuals, people are no longer fighting alienation but a kind of total dispossession.

PP: When small nations fight for their existence, how is that a dispossession?

JB: Because they are already virtually condemned. They are in the ebbing of identity. They are no longer in a battle for an ascending identity, for a sovereignty. They are fighting with their backs to the wall and for a cause which is not glorious, because identity is a weak value, a neutral value. They are simply fighting to prove they exist, or sometimes even, like the Armenians, to prove they no longer exist, that they have been massacred.

PP: On identity I can agree. But history! On page 23 of *The Illusion of the End*, you write:

> [W]e no longer make history. We have become reconciled with it and protect it like an endangered masterpiece. Times have changed. We have today a perfectly pious 'vision' of the Revolution, cast in terms of the Rights of Man. Not even a nostalgic vision, but one recycled in the terms of postmodern intellectual comfort. A vision which allows us to eliminate Saint-Just from the *Dictionnaire de la Révolution*. 'Overrated rhetoric', says François Furet, perfect historian of the repentance of the Terror and of glory.

Does this pious vision of the Revolution apply to contemporary historical consciousness?

JB: It's on the way to becoming our common consciousness. The cleaning-up of the French Revolution, the assertion that the Revolution failed because it ended in terror – this kind of repentance and retrospective cleansing is merely revisionism.

But it's no exception. It's incredible how everything today is of the order of cleansing. The museification of events, the rehabilitations and commemorations, are all aimed at this laundering of events. That the powers that be should do such work is their affair, but that intellectuals and those who were actors in history should afford themselves the cynical luxury of carrying out this cleansing is scandalous. Do you know a country which isn't a product of the ravages of history? History isn't made by historical rationality alone. The societies which haven't allowed themselves violent, extravagant events have remained in a cataleptic state. What is it with these fine souls rectifying history? I find historical Pharisaism repugnant. . . .

PP: Yet you were an '*intellectuel engagé*'.

JB: More *dégagé*. The so-called committed intellectuals have had so little influence on politics, in spite of their reflections on the matter. The concept of history, such as comes into general use in the nineteenth century, corresponds to the moment when we were beginning to leave history. It's always the same. It's at the moment when we begin to intellectualize a phenomenon that in reality it disappears. With Sartre we managed to maintain a kind of nostalgia, but it was already over. 'Committed' theory is always a desperate attempt to reconstruct what's on the point of vanishing.

PP: Foucault thought it was possible to make a diagnosis of the present.

JB: Diagnosis no longer has the objective meaning it had in Foucault. I don't believe this diagnosis is still possible. Is it possible today to record things objectively? I doubt it. Scientists hardly make diagnoses of objects – which are ungraspable – any longer, but they build up all kinds of hypotheses. Can we do any more than that? I'm not sure we can. One may analyse situations with the same intelligence as Sartre. But that's a level of intellectual gratification. And yet the other level remains, the level of hypotheses. Is it an interesting hypothesis to reconsider history in the light of a generic concept? I don't think so.

PP: Let's concede that. You no longer believe in history as a rational concept, you no longer believe in the promises of history. But what about the criticism of the world in the name of its own promises, as Adorno put it? Do you still believe in that? Do you still, with Gilles Deleuze, believe 'not in another world, but in the bond between man and the world, in love or in life'?[2]

JB: The world, if we take it as we find it, has no history. It has, at best, a destiny, but how are we to know what that is? How are we to know if what's in play is the destination of the *genre humain* as it was born at the beginning of its history, a humanity whose genealogy we can trace out, a humanity that is perpetually ascending? What has changed is that the stakes have shifted to the level of the species, not the historico-cultural entity. It's the destiny of the species that's in play. Now, it's much more difficult to believe in a project of the species. Even in our own day, nine-tenths of humanity is outside history, outside a system of interpretation and recording which was born with modern times and will disappear. History is a kind of luxury Western societies have afforded themselves. It's 'their' history. The fact that it seems to be disappearing is unfortunate for us, but it allows destiny, which has always been the lot of other cultures, to take over. The other cultures have never lacked destiny, whereas we, in our Western societies, are bereft of it.

PP: Bergson didn't have to deal with unemployment and the crisis of work. There are social syndromes, such as the disintegration of work and of wage-based society, which are of the order of unprecedented changes. Isn't this a new historico-political task?

JB: Don't capital and labour have the same destiny? Can we describe work today as a productive force and as the basis of wealth? So long as labour was experienced by the majority of human beings as an alienation, it was possible to allot it a subversive role. Man faced up to the machines as best he could. It was said that they were alienating, and man tried to free himself from them. But in our new logistics of man–machine interaction, we're no longer dealing with labour. Man and the machine are interfaced. There's no longer any subject of labour. There's an operation. We're no longer in a situation of transcendent, vertical confrontation. We are, rather, in a horizontal situation of functioning and networks. Nowadays, someone who works is pretty much a corpse they can't manage to get rid of. The System would quite like to get rid of it, but it can't quite manage the trick, and the suffering workers don't want to lose their *raison d'être* either. This is paradoxical. But in the overall picture now, labour no longer figures as a ruptural energy, nor even as a source of wealth: it's merely a form of identity claim. Modern technologies, all this high-tech equipment, are no longer so much extensions of man, as McLuhan used to say, but human beings are now becoming, rather, a kind of extension of the logistical system – and then what comeback can there be? How can they refer to their own labour, since this no longer has any true definition? There's no longer really a price, or value, of labour. Labour is caught up so much in multiply interconnected networks, like information, that it can't even really be evaluated. It's caught in that speculative form of work that is employment, which is no longer part of a social contract, but quoted now as an economic indicator. And it isn't just workers who are in this position. There are no more Sartre-style group-subjects. Even the capitalists, the bosses, the strategists are no longer in the position of subjects, any more than intellectuals are. They're just playing extra time. . . .

PP: Paul Virilio, who is more Christian than you, thinks intellectuals have a duty to resist the global forms of domination. They are, he says, in the position of the painters who resisted photography in the last century. Aren't you, in your way, a resistance fighter waiting to go over to the offensive?

JB: We worked together for a long time with Virilio, very closely and without any problems. At the time I didn't see his Christianity surface. It surprises me, because his books deny the very possibility of a morality of resistance. His analysis of the cyberworld is intransigent, inexorable and, if I may venture the term, *fatale*. I find it remarkable and very fine. But I don't believe in what he sets against that world. I hope he believes in it. He puts himself in an apocalyptic position, in the position of an anti-apocalyptic prophet, while remaining convinced that the worst may occur. In the end we diverged on this point, as I don't believe in this real apocalypse. I don't believe in realism, at any event, nor in a linear maturing of the apocalypse. Ultimately, if we could hope for this total accident, then the only thing would be to precipitate it; we shouldn't resist it.

The coming of the virtual itself is our apocalypse, and it deprives us of the real event of the apocalypse. Such is our paradoxical situation, but we have to push the paradox to the limit. And Virilio in fact does this, while reserving a fallback argument for himself.

PP: What do you mean by saying 'we have to push the paradox to the limit'?

JB: Recognizing that the movement of the system itself is irreversible, that there's no possible get-out within the logic of the system. That logic really is global in the sense that it has absorbed all negativities, including the humanist, universalist resistance, etc. Pushing to the limit means acknowledging this irreversibility and pushing it to the limit of its possibilities, to the point of collapse. Bringing it to saturation point, to the point where the system itself creates the accident. Thought contributes to this acceleration. It anticipates its end. This is the provocative function of thought: having no illusions as to its critical function or to its 'commitment', but giving all it's got to imagining the end.

PP: Why are you so keen on this notion of irreversibility? It's odd. The globalization of the economy doesn't lead irrevocably to the homogenization of the world; it doesn't prevent us from reconstructing politics either, does it?

JB: You can always fight the global in the name of the universal. I prefer the direct confrontation between globalization and all the antagonistic singularities. To maintain the humanist mediations at all costs is to put an obstacle in the way of that confrontation in its radicality.

PP: To what extent is your theory a justifiable response to the ordeal of globalization?

JB: I don't claim that. I claim that theory must anticipate.

We have to recognize the clear-out being effected by the system. There's no redeeming of history. I believe it's better to focus on the radical originality of a situation. The thought which flows from this has a chance of being itself more original. This is the opposite of repentance. The judgement of the intellectual world is too often the judgement of repentance.

PP: Your obsession would have pleased Witkiewicz!

JB: It's true there's no longer any history 'in progress'. But we have to distinguish between the event and history. History assumes a continuity, an explanatory principle. By contrast, what happens may run against history, against politics. 'Sixty-eight seemed to me to be a discontinuity of that type and, in this sense, a harbinger. Since then, all that has really constituted an event has been done against politics and history. I've been accused of being on the side of the system on the pretext that I describe the perverse effects of these things. That's wrong. Underlying what I write is . . . not hope, but events irreducible to the involutive logic of global systems. The only nihilistic analysis of events is the pious one. Every radical analysis is stunningly optimistic!

Chapter 2
'A World Too Many'

Philippe Petit: 'We can no longer speak Evil. All we can do is discourse on human rights,' you write in *The Transparency of Evil*.[3] The quest for the end of evil, the aim of achieving its final abolition, which in the past – as Alain Besançon argues[4] – was handed over to the Communist and Nazi movements to pursue, is currently blighting democratic societies! Suppressing evil and eradicating violence has become, in its turn, the unavowed dream of the democracies. What does 'being able to speak evil' mean for you? To point it out, to name it, to recognize it as such?

Jean Baudrillard: Pointing it out as a localizable object is not what I mean. For that, you'd have to be referring to a value system. Now, evil is more a form than a value. I don't define it in a moral sense, nor, for that matter, in an immoral sense. Before being an immorality, evil is first an antagonistic principle. We can, however, retain from the religious vision of evil the idea of negation, illusion, destruction. From this point of view, evil is an unbinding agent. In fact, good lies in the clear opposition between good and evil. Evil lies in the lack of any distinction between the two. So long as good and evil can trade off against each other, the one being dialectically linked to the other, we are in the universe of good. Evil lies either before or beyond the opposition between good and evil. Or – to put it another way – good is simply the part of the iceberg above water, the submerged nine-tenths of which are the evil portion. There might be said, then, to be no substantive difference between the two, only a difference of visibility and transparency.

PP: 'Anything that purges the accursed share [*part maudite*] in itself signs its own death warrant. This is the theorem of the accursed share. The energy of the accursed share, and its violence, are expressions of the principle of Evil,' we read on page 106 of *The Transparency of Evil*. In so far as our societies stubbornly seek to drive out evil as though it were a microbe, they run the risk, you say, of 'a catastrophe caused by a thoroughgoing backlash, just as any organism that hunts down and eliminates its germs, bacteria, parasites or other biological antagonists risks metastasis and cancer – in other words, it is threatened by a voracious positivity of its own cells. . . .' What substantive difference is there between the accursed share according to Bataille, and Baudrillard's version?

JB: In Bataille's conception, the accursed share is something which cannot be exchanged in accordance with conventional exchange procedures, and must therefore be sacrificed if a form of functional equilibrium is to be recovered. Primitive societies have two cycles, two levels. There is routine exchange and there is what goes into the cycle of sacrifice; Bataille says this latter is expended in vain (though not really, since it re-establishes the equilibrium). There is a fantastic excess, which comes from the sun or from love, and that energy must be expended. When this can no longer be brought into play, the group is in peril. The problem is that, in our societies, we can no longer speak evil; we are no longer able to use this accursed share sacrificially, this part which corresponds to the fact that too much is produced, too many signs, too many goods, too much wealth – and perhaps also too many individuals. Bataille is still functionalist to the extent that once it has gone into the cycle of sacrifice, this accursed share allows a society to reproduce and perpetuate itself. This has given rise to the most vulgar interpretations. It's been argued that in consumer societies waste is the equivalent of potlatch, and everything that has no economic rationality has been put down as a kind of accursed share.

The unconscious can be made out to be the accursed share of the human soul, and so on. I prefer to keep to the idea that it is central to evil and its eccentricity.

PP: When you say there's 'too much wealth', does that mean that in your system there's no place for what Paul Ricoeur calls an ethics of concern? There are too many children dying of hunger, too many poor people?

JB: The question is one of determining whether misery isn't accompanied by an ethics of concern which would merely double the misery – as is the case with every moral value in the Nietzschean age of suspicion. We speak of nothing but destitution and misery, and the international community pretends to mobilize, but the extermination follows its course. We are under a curse without knowing it, engaged in a process of collective disappearance which we ourselves are involuntarily bringing about. The fact is that the growth of our societies is veering off towards a form of global disqualification and excrescence that is out of anyone's control. We're up to our necks in this excessive culture of material production, but that's not enough to make it an 'accursed share'. The unrestrained growth of everything doesn't give rise to sacrifice, merely to waste. For there to be sacrifice, things have to be yielded up to evil, not simply to misfortune. We have to come to terms with the inhuman, with an inhuman form we no longer wish to accept or recognize at all today – failing which, we fall into a total dehumanization by effacing this necessary relation between the human and the inhuman. We see so many fine souls setting themselves up today as prophets of misery, but no one to speak evil. Now, the human shows up in a moving and mysterious way only through those who are bereft of it. The idea of the human can come only from elsewhere, not from itself. The inhuman alone can bear witness to it. When the human attempts to define itself by excluding the inhuman, it becomes a mockery. When it aspires to realize its own concept in humanism and humanitarian action, it immediately surpasses itself in violence and absurdity. Thought lives only on the margins of the human, at the asymptotic limit of the inhuman – the human ironically hidden behind the inhuman – and the opposite: the inhuman ironically peering out through the human, just like the object ironically peering out through the subject. Transparence of evil.[5]

For this defence and illustration of evil [*le mal*], as opposed to misfortune [*le malheur*], one is immediately accused of irresponsibility, of being reactionary, nihilistic. Now, to speak evil is merely to say, hypothetically, that its principle is currently being realized, without anyone knowing it but with everyone having a part in it. It's to speak the transparence of evil, it's to denounce all this denial of the accursed share and the evidence of evil, this denial of the inhuman.

PP: The problem is that that theorem depends on the idea that the principle of evil is coextensive with its energy. You have in the past taken the example of New York as an archetype of non-negative survival, as a model of the energetic principle of survival, in which everyone, from addicts to 'golden boys', is part of the general survival of the city. In so far as we are not speaking of a positive energy here – since, in your conception, true energy comes from dissolution – does this mean that the rise and rise of the accursed share is irreversible?

JB: Let's say that the irreversibility of this growth and this expenditure might be said to be itself the evil. Exponentiality itself is like a curse, a fatality. Or, rather, a parody of the accursed share and fate. For what is inexorably happening to us is not the fatal. What is coming our way with globalization might, rather, be termed the 'viral', an outgrowth of the banal. Globalization is the automatic realization of the world, the automatic writing of the world. The 'fatal' is the opposite; it's the fact that the system devours itself – that, by its irreversibility, it engenders a kind of total reversion of things. What is fatal – and therefore fortunate – is the system's illusion about itself. The fatal in that sense is the opposite of this undertaking of the perfecting of the world, its automation and technologization, which go together with the irresistible advance of good, of a world purged of death and negativity, an operational world.

PP: Let's take the example of revisionism and negationism which you mention. Is there really anything more to be said about these two monsters?

JB: The idea that the extermination did not take place is clearly inadmissible. But the opposite idea, which dominates thinking today – that negationism is immoral – is also a mistake. Of course, historically, the negationists are wrong inasmuch as they wish to establish a different historical truth. But their proposition as an actual utterance needs to be deciphered. The mere fact of that proposition being possible signifies that, in the real time in which we live, this historical time of the Holocaust no longer exists, and it is impossible to revive it in a living memory because we are no longer in the same time. What's worse than the act of saying the Holocaust did not exist is the fact of having to prove the Holocaust and having to defend its existence as a moral – if not, indeed, ideological and political – truth.

PP: Claude Lanzmann has managed to show the extermination process. You say both that 'Auschwitz and extermination' are inexpiable and that Auschwitz is no longer a part of our present. Isn't that contradictory?

JB: Auschwitz can be reactivated, recollected in terms of archives, made a museum piece, presented for consumption in an un-present that is ours, in which everything passes into the instantaneousness of real time, dissolves in that instantaneousness. This is our fate [*fatalité*]. And in this sphere, Faurisson's proposition can be advanced; at the very least, the conditions of possibility for that proposition exist today. Because the very definition of past events is changing, and poses a problem. When one says this, one is accused of taking sides and speaking evil. And one cannot speak evil without being, in the eyes of the dominant thinking which is a thinking based in good, a traitor and an impostor. It is, however, true that memory, like many other things, has been abolished by the structure of real time, and that it's useless to inveigh against this in the name of a morality of history.

PP: Let's stick with this topic. Staying with *The Transparency of Evil*, on page 90 we find the following passage:

> It is really only because we have disappeared politically and historically today (and therein lies our problem) that we seek to prove that we died between 1940 and 1945,

at Auschwitz or in Hiroshima – which at least makes for a *strong* history. We are like the Armenians, who wear themselves out trying to prove that they were massacred in 1917 – a proof that is unattainable, useless, yet in some sense vital. It is because philosophy too has disappeared today (and therein lies *its* problem, for how can something live if it has disappeared?) that it seeks to demonstrate that it was definitively compromised with Heidegger, or rendered aphasic by Auschwitz.

I would be more nuanced than you on this latter point, but we'll let that pass. I should like you to clarify your idea of disappearance. Is it because we're living in the age of 'real time', under its tyranny, that there's disappearance, or is it because real time is our destiny?

JB: Real time is our mode of extermination today. It's every bit the equal of the other. It isn't as bloody, but it's a form of the inhuman. The final solution was at Auschwitz, but it was also in the film *Holocaust*, which retraced the memory, and thus gave the illusion of memory. When you add repentance and moral good conscience to a traumatic event, in a way you sanction it and take its ruptural energy from it. It's the same with Hiroshima. An exhibition was held showing photos of the city before the bomb, of the city annihilated, and of Hiroshima as it is today. Now, it's true that Hiroshima is a city reborn, but this new Hiroshima is also a part of its being definitively wiped out. The traumatic event has been whitewashed. All archives are whitewashing devices. The event is distanced from us once and for all by the very means available to us for remembering it. This is a form of fatality. But who are we to make responsible for it? We're all party to it.

PP: What, for you, is the exact content of this real time?

JB: If you wish to give a meaning to this contradictory expression (since real time abolishes every real dimension of time), it would be the possibility of making everything present in an instant. It's the time of immediate realization, of global dissemination, of action at a distance. Which abolishes any present–past–future sequence, and hence any consequentiality. Real time is a sort of fourth dimension in which all other dimensions are abolished. The future is absorbed because it has already taken place in real time. So it doesn't have the time to take place. And the past, for its part, doesn't have the time to have taken place. As for the present, it's only ever the present of the screens. So: real time is a kind of fourth dimension, the dimension of the virtual, substituted for the real, which is the real's absolute realization. Hence there's no more possibility for the real to emerge, since there's a precession of the virtual, as once there was a precession of models and simulacra. The real is, fundamentally, an unstable state. It has doubtless always been an unstable state, which has benefited for over two centuries from a favourable conjunction. One in which there has been the possibility of producing the same effects from the same causes. It's all that which has been deconstructed. It's the relation between cause and effect which has become indiscernible, or has perhaps even reversed. Between the initial conditions and the final conditions we no longer know what happens. Real time is a bit like this: the collision between the opposite poles of the future and the past, of the subject and the object. The collision between a question and an answer. These merge together and are thus wiped out. It's an insurmountable reality, not only in the sciences, but in the general ordering of our existences.

PP: You admit, however, that writing can be one of the forms of resistance to real time?

JB: There is, at any rate, nothing more contrary to thought and writing than their real-time operation on a screen or a computer. Writing depends on the strict separation between the screen and the text, the image and the text. It requires a gaze, a distance. Even with the typewriter, I can still see the page, I have a physical relationship to writing. Whereas on the screen, even if you're dealing with a text, you're in the visual (which is not even a sensory image, but a kind of virtual reality of thought and writing). You're immersed in an interactive, even intersensory, relation. Now, writing's never an interaction. It's not only a resistance to real time, but something else: a singularity. I wouldn't say, as Virilio does, that it's a resistance, a defence of the old world and slowness. It might be said, rather, to be a form of singularity, a thing which doesn't conform. It's another game, in the sense that it's the invention of another, antagonistic, world. It's not the defence of a world that might have existed, the defence of the book and of meaning and culture as values. Writing has a more offensive action. It constitutes an event in a world where there are no longer any events because everything's in the programme. Writing isn't an act of resistance, but it is an act irreducible to the general functioning. Other things fall into this category too.

PP: If you speak of the invention of another world, then the world isn't totally lost?

JB: I would say, like Rimbaud, that we're no longer in the world. With the con-struction of a parallel, virtual world substituted for our own, we're no longer in the world. Being in the world has become an improbable eventuality. Simply to say 'I exist' isn't serious. Being in the world isn't being present in the world, nor being iden-tical to oneself. It's playing on complicity, absence, illusion, distance from the world.

PP: Your delight in playing with language seems to increase with every day that passes. . . .

JB: The fact is that it's not a familiar form you can use and abuse, but something alien which has to be seduced. No question of slipping something by it. You have to surprise it and let it surprise you.

PP: You admit, then, that it's possible to 'recover speech'. What I don't understand is why you deny this possibility to Primo Levi, Robert Antelme, to all the literature of the camps, which has a greatness in that it has exhumed the suffering of those who have disappeared, and allowed the survivors to convey their torment to us?

JB: I don't deny anyone anything. There are narratives which don't partake of that whitewashing process we've been speaking of. They are organically part of the event. They are still present traces of the event. I simply say that we're in a world where it's becoming necessary to prove what has happened, which is paradoxical, and proof is unfortunately increasingly impossible. That fact, unacceptable as one may find it, has to be interpreted. We're abandoned to a system which no longer allows us to recapture an objectivity, a historicity of things. That's how it is. If there's something to be done, it certainly isn't to deny negationism, to drive it out with good conscience.

PP: Surely if no journalist had spoken about Garaudy's book, the one published by La Vieille Taupe,[6] it wouldn't have been read. What's your view on this?

JB: We would have to question the part played by all the media in this. They don't proceed in an ideological way, but functionally. And their mode of functioning – in real time, as we were saying – tends to propagate this un-presencing of memory. They do their work. The question of what would happen if they didn't speak of Garaudy is of the order of magical thinking. The media speak; that's what they're there for. They transmit the virus. They are the virus. Which means they exert an extraordinary fascination by way of catastrophes, accidents, violence, and all that sort of thing. It's black magic which plays best.

All virtual technologies propagate undecidability. But is it the virtual technologies which propagate undecidability, or our undecidable universe which manufactures the technologies of the virtual? It's undecidable! It's the same with the media. They aren't responsible, they propagate irresponsibility, which is our mode of collective solidarity today. Citizens don't consciously decide to watch television. They do it by a kind of attraction, intoxication. Each one is an intermediate point in the circuit, or on that Moebius strip of news and information. I have a notion that all this virtual machinery doesn't have information, knowledge or any genuine coming together as its real dimension, but an inclination to disappear. All that the new technologies have brought us have been types of images in which you immerse yourself with the possibility of modifying them. How can anyone think that you can enter a video image to make of it what you will, and that there will still be facts, events or values which can resist this electronic immersion? Everything will pass into this real sensory deprivation chamber that is the screens and the networks.

PP: You say we're no longer in a world where we can prove something. Yet, at the same time, we spend our time trying to apportion responsibility, finding people to blame. The contaminated blood affair is an illustration of this. . . .

JB: It's reactional. A network is made to refer on from one element to another. There's no possibility of stopping it. It's viral. You can't either 'freeze' on an image or 'freeze' on responsibility. Everything which circulates brings with it the impossibility of really identifying an actor with his act. You try hard to find coherent sequences, causes and effects. But, taken overall, there's no longer any law or mode of equivalence. Now, responsibility is a mode of equivalence and exchange of moral norms, one of the ethical forms we're looking for today. A desperate undertaking, admittedly, but that's just the point: the more hopeless it is, the more ethical committees there will be.

PP: The happy conjunction between idea and reality no longer being on the agenda in your writings, how can we avoid suspecting you of nihilism? In combating the illusion of reality as you do, do you not fear retreating into value-relativism and taking your desire for disappearance for reality itself?

JB: I don't think so. In no way is there any question of a differential or relativism of values in my modest challenge to the illusion of reality. There *is* a challenge to reality: what becomes of thought if you place yourself at these extreme limits, at the level of extreme phenomena. Is there still thought at that level? There isn't exactly an answer. If thought is a challenge, it owes it to itself to be experimental. What I do is more of a thought experiment which tries to explore an unknown field by other rules. This doesn't mean it's 'nihilistic' in the sense in which nihilism means there are no longer any values, no longer any reality, but only signs: the accusation of nihilism and imposture always relates to that point. But if you take nihilism in the strong sense, the sense of a nothing-based thinking, a thinking which might start out from the axiom 'why is there nothing rather than something?' – overturning the fundamental philosophical question, the question of being: 'why is there something rather than nothing?' – then I don't mind being called a nihilist.

I make the hypothesis that the world exists as it is, that you can take it for real and intelligible in its internal functioning, but that otherwise, taken overall, there's no general equivalent of this world and, as a consequence, no intelligibility to it, and no objective evaluation of it. It can't be exchanged for something else. It's of the order of impossible exchange. This is the world's fundamental uncertainty principle. If I consider the economy, for example, I can't deny there's a principle of economic reality, structures of economic exchange. But the economic, taken overall, can't be exchanged for anything. There's no equivalent for the economic sphere as such. In this sense it is, strictly speaking, unintelligible in terms of radical thought. Radical thought doesn't annihilate the real – how could it? It puts it out of play, out of equivalence. Whereas dialectical thought and critical thought are part of the field of exchange – including, possibly, market exchange – radical thought situates itself in the zone of impossible exchange, of non-equivalence, of the unintelligible, the undecidable.

PP: I well understand your concern to uncouple the real from the rational. That's a kind of thumbing your nose at philosophy which has too often tried to unite being and thought. But don't you, in turn, fall back into the fiction of the unity of science and philosophy? Where does your radical thought situate itself precisely: alongside, opposite, or in the wake of science and philosophy?

JB: Elsewhere, but just before the end. That's to say, in the paroxystic phase. The interesting moment is the moment of paroxysm, which isn't the final moment, but the moment just before the end. Paroxystic thought is in next-to-last position, ahead of the extreme point where there will be nothing more to be said. It's not scientific because science, as a system of exchange, of information, of storage, claims to provide a final and objective meaning. Now, if there's no overarching representation of the world which gives it a meaning, then there can't be a science either that would be the key to the whole story. It's the same with the human sciences. The fact that disciplines like economics or history, and all sciences in general, have an internal principle of intelligibility as a function of their postulates, but nowhere else, means that they are increasingly unsettled by uncertainty. This unintelligibility in the last instance impacts back on their internal functioning. The so-called exact sciences don't escape this, since they, too, are on the fringes of this undecidability between subject and object.

PP: You write: 'No one believes in the real any more, nor in the evidence of their own life.' What a verdict! This is good news for Jean Baudrillard, isn't it?

JB: Indeed, from a Stoic viewpoint, it's futile to wish to add belief to the objectality, the radicality, of the event! Belief is a weak value. My hypothesis is that, behind the belief systems by which we fabulate the real and give it a meaning, there is in everyone (and this isn't a question of intelligence or consciousness) a radical empiricism which means that fundamentally no one believes in this idea of reality. Everyone has a radicality threshold which gives them a purchase on the world outside of their ideologies and beliefs. Not to add to desire the pathos of desire. Not to add to belief the pathos of belief. Not to add hope to hope. All these values divert us from thought. The Stoics knew this. The important thing is to find distance and freedom from these overlays. To try to sweep away this subjective or collective ideological proliferation.

PP: That puts me in mind of a remark by Laruelle in *Biographie de l'homme ordinaire* in which he says that what counts isn't to grasp [*begreifen*] the world, but to know how to reject it in a kind of Stoic indifference.[7]

JB: Yes, to clear the decks around the object of thought, as it were, as one does around material objects, without making it exist, or interpreting it, in advance. There's a moment when you can grasp the object or the world in terms of appearance, not in terms of the production of a world already fashioned in the image of thought, just before it's rigged out with a finality, just before it 'comes to an end' (once again, the paroxystic moment).

PP: What status do you accord to thought?

JB: You can, on the one hand, imagine that it plays a regulative role, that in a certain sense it tempers the illusion of the world. It might be said to give us something to live by, by creating around us a rational configuration, an imagining of the world in which the species can find its own reflection. Then it would have a positive mirror function, and would contribute to an informing of the world – that is to say, to ever greater rationality, and less and less entropy. That's the ideal, idealist vision. Or, alternatively, it's a challenge, a trap for reality to fall into, a way of moving more swiftly to the end, getting more quickly to the final goal, whatever that is, and going beyond. And so more of a catastrophic form, a play of appearance and disappearance, which thinks the world as illusion or hypothesizes that the world has, in a way, already disappeared. Then it works in secret, at the heart of the rational system, on this ultra-rationalization of the world, the catastrophic form of the world's precipitation towards its end. Thought plays a very ironic role here. It's been presented as a positive strategy, a rational factor, but no doubt it always plays a double game. Perhaps it's simply a form of bug, of virus, which develops inside the system itself and which, by virtue of the very proliferation of the system, is destabilizing it from the inside. This is the more interesting version in the current conjuncture.

PP: I can see your image of thought, as Deleuze might have said, a bit more clearly. You said it's a thought which has a radical uncertainty as its reference, which no longer has truth as its horizon. I should like to know, before you give some examples of your thesis, what exact status you accord to the real. You're fond of saying that the virtual, in which we're steeped, no longer produces reality. I shall turn the question around and ask it of yourself: do you produce reality?

JB: I am, of course, party, by the use of discourse, to reflexive thought, so I'm also playing a double game. Deleuze says we manufacture concepts. It's work. One doesn't manufacture a mode of explanation or truth, but a form of vision, of style, in order to see and decipher. That thought functions, and we make it function. But I wonder if the counter-finality of that thought doesn't function in spite of us. And, when you think, it's possible that in an almost occult way there's a kind of principle of evil active behind that thinking, a demonic dimension. Perhaps unconscious

37

actors are more active in the process than actors of the thinking variety. If thought is a function, it's a truly ambivalent and, I would even say, antagonistic one. Something escapes us in this. It's both grey matter and dark matter. There's an obscure mass stalking the whole of philosophy, together with a radical and silent disillusionment, which no longer allow rational thought to maintain a transcendence, a hope, an ideal. All those things did have their basis, and it isn't a question of denying them retrospectively, but something else has happened. Now, thought is on both sides. And this is disconcerting.

PP: Thought is on both sides. Does that mean it can be said to have killed reality, and at the same time might turn out to be against the murder?

JB: Yes, it's the murder weapon. Even as it's disappearing, the real is a mystery. Why is there reality, or why is there not? From this breaking of the matter/antimatter symmetry, the philosophical question begins: why is there something rather than nothing? Beyond the privileging of the material world, this elusive thing we left aside comes back to haunt our dreams and the question becomes, as I said, why is there nothing rather than something? An anti-philosophical question if you like, or is it the final form of the philosophical question? The philosophical version is: 'There is being, and what is not being is nothing'; it doesn't exist. Evil doesn't exist. This is the theological, philosophical vision. Evil has no existence, evil isn't real. In my view the opposite would be true now. It's the something that's a problem, and one wonders how something has been able to aspire to being and have the slightest chance of discoursing upon itself. That's the mystery! A reality which is tending to disappear today under the very violence of its interpretation, and to give way to this questioning about the void, about the status of the real itself. With wave mechanics and quantum physics our universe ceases to obey immutable laws. There are no longer any true laws, and we find ourselves faced with a definitive indeterminacy. The problem is how, at the heart of that indeterminacy, laws can appear and the reality effect emerge. This is where the problem turns around. It isn't the nothing – the other of the real, the other of rationality – which is a problem, but the real itself.

Chapter 3
The Great Game

Philippe Petit: In your book *Symbolic Exchange and Death*, there's lengthy discussion of old age, death, and what might be called the culture of death. You relate that culture to the law of capital, and write:

> If capital, and its Marxist critique, no longer exist, that is because the law of value has gone over into the self-management of survival in all its forms. If the cemetery no longer exists, that is because modern cities as a whole have taken over that function. They are dead cities and cities of death. And if the great operational metropolis is the finished form of a whole culture, then quite simply ours is a culture of death.

Would you write the same thing today?

Jean Baudrillard: In *Symbolic Exchange and Death*, death was a figure of the reversibility of life and death, the symbolic being always a sign of the reversibility of things. The culture of death is a dead end, a true death, whereas death taken in the symbolic sense is quite different. It's impossible to remove this ambiguity. A number of terms wind around on themselves, and sometimes take on a negative, catastrophic air, whereas they are in fact figures of inversion. Rather than death, we should speak today of extermination. This isn't necessarily a violent, physical extermination but, rather, the coming of a spectral, virtual universe, a devitalized, lobotomized form. So we're not talking about death as murder or destiny. We're talking, rather, about the absence of destiny. We no longer live against the horizon of death – that is to say, the horizon of the symbolic murder, which would give a fantastic energy. We live in slow, endemic, viral elimination. We could be said to be in a society of exclusion, of foreclosure, of death. A lethal state.

PP: In *Symbolic Exchange and Death*, you are – if I dare put it this way – still a sociologist. Some pages aren't very far removed from Philippe Ariès's writing on the same subject. It seems now that that sociology doesn't interest you at all. . . .

JB: No, I've never been a sociologist in that sense. I moved away very early on from the sociology of institutions, of law, of social structures, from those approaches based on the idea of an imagining of the social, of its transcendence. My object might rather be said to be a society losing its transcendence, from which the social, the very idea of the social, has withdrawn. Hence the concept of mass, of silent majority. The masses are no longer a sociological concept. They are a kind of amorphous agency, a sort of silent potency or anti-potency, an indefinable antimatter of the social.

In a way, I prefer anthropology to sociology. It seems to me that anthropology's a bit further removed than sociology from this social realism. It's closer to the metamorphosis of the species, in a more acute, virulent form than at the level of sociality.

What I object to in sociology is, in fact, its realism, its taking of the social for the social and its failure to envisage that it might, at a particular moment, be an opportunity, a dream, a utopia, a contradiction – in short, something other than the social – its acting as though the social dimension were given. This is what I would term its deep-seated Rousseauism. There's nothing less certain than that man is a social being; that he might cease to be so is a possibility to be considered. Anthropology can be Rousseauist too. Indeed, it was even more Rousseauist at its origins, but it's closer to getting its object in perspective. Some anthropologists have even ended up leaving alone the primitive tribes they discovered for fear of destroying and destructuring them, preferring to forgo an object that's out of reach, an object forever impossible since it vanishes into knowledge itself. A more interesting, more original situation, and one which therefore links up, at some point, with the originality of its object. Closer to a primal scene of the object than sociology, which has made the incontestable, self-evident existence of the social into a kind of postulate, and for which the social is proven by its very existence, a tautology which unfortunately undergirds all our human sciences today.

PP: If sociology goes out of the window at the point where you bring out the foreclosure of death, what is left? This brings to mind a passage in Cioran's *Histoire et utopie* in which he defends fanaticism and criticizes the flabbiness of liberal democracies.[8] Speaking of the Russian world, he writes that the Slavic countries, in their noble blindness, are the only ones in the world to put their faith in the destinies of the West, and he adds, before outlining what he terms 'zones of vitality': 'These Balkan societies all still have a biological basis one would seek in vain in the West.' When you say we have foreclosed death and exhausted our vital resources, isn't it the case that you're ultimately sorry to see this primitivism, these zones of vitality, this degree of instinct, go? Might not your antimodernism be a kind of revolt against the supposed decadence of the West?

JB: There's certainly some disenchantment in the air. Having said that, the idea of the decadence of the West is part of its cultural language. The West has always delighted in imagining its own death. I don't seek to locate the counterpoint to the West. That there is an alternative I don't doubt, but it's not in space: it's first and foremost metaphysical, it's in forms. You can find it running through Eastern societies, or those of Africa and Latin America. The problem for us Westerners is not the problem of an alternative, but of the alterity we have lost and which all those who are copying us are also losing. We have lost alterity and death. And, unlike Cioran, I don't think the dream of a vital absolute will bring them back to us. It's not in terms of vital instinct that Russia holds its own against the West. It's simply that the Russians have a culture of death that is much more forceful, much more virulent than ours.

PP: I'd like to tie this remark in with something you said recently at Beaubourg on the spirit of the age. 'Life is no longer forming,' you said, referring to Jean Rostand. How do you make sense of such an entropy and such an exhaustion of the *élan vital*?

JB: I don't make sense of it! I quite like Rostand's idea, but as a hypothesis. From the moment you're in a universe where the die is cast, you find yourself in an infinite combinatory of an entropic type. With the separation between matter and antimatter achieved, and this latter eternally elusive, we're in a finite material world where, in this sense, matter is no longer being created. This corpus, which – though infinite in its complexity – is finite, but separated from antimatter, is doomed to entropy. Similarly, any given system, if it manages to circumscribe itself and to exclude all radical otherness, begins to devour itself. This goes for all organizations, all institutions, for the biomass in general, but also for the logomass, for language. Everything which tries to lay down for itself the definitive postulates for its operation begins to rush towards its completion. Everything tends to complete itself, to accomplish itself in its being, which is a distillation of death.

PP: In 1976 you still spoke of modern rationality; today you tend to speak simply of thought. You said a moment ago that Western thought had contaminated the world, and it was that which was making us devour and exhaust ourselves. Shouldn't we interrogate the status of thought? Wouldn't it be possible, in spite of this menacing entropy, to carry out a kind of Copernican revolution of thought, and shake off the straitjacket? Some thinkers, like François Laruelle, manage to do this. What's the type of configuration that would, in your opinion, best suit your philosophical objectives [*objectifs de pensée*]?

JB: This is a basic problem. There would no doubt be a distinction to be made from a thinking built upon the rational order, a thinking organized in terms of description, limits and definitions. That is looking for a balance, a dialectic. It's trying to give an account of the world. It is, in principle, exchangeable against a dream of transforming the world to which it contributes. That style of thinking seems to me doomed to be caught in its own trap. It always ends in simulation, where the crucial question remains: 'Does the sign refer to meaning, or is it merely a reference to itself and a promotion of the sign as sign?' Simulation and the virtual being an extension and not a Copernican revolution, as you put it, that style of thinking has managed to produce the illusion of an intelligible world. We have to knock that thinking from its pedestal and pay attention to what is ex-centred, eccentric. If we look at it this way, it's no longer we who think the world, but the world which thinks us. It's the world which restores a metamorphosis of forms in which thought itself is caught in a dynamic that is no longer its own. We no longer know very precisely what role it plays in this, if it is a force for acceleration or inertia. We become the objects of thought, but objects of a thought which no longer belongs to us, which is no longer the thought of the subject. What I wanted to do was to explore this kind of thought which has become centrifugal, a kind of extreme veering-off beyond its objectives. Does it link up somewhere with the other style of thought, including scientific thought, scientific experimentation? Does it meet up with a form of radical uncertainty? I don't know. Let's say that we manufacture a double of the world which substitutes itself for the world. We generate the confusion between the world and its double.

PP: What do you mean by forms of the world?

JB: It's a kind of symbolic circulation, of reversibility and linkage, of constellations, as in the primitive representations of the world where animals, plants, human beings and the elements link with and act against each other. This is how it is with the sexes in seduction, and with the poetic form, which is the form of the anamorphosis of language into its scattered elements.

PP: Does this play of forms have anything to do with what Kostas Axelos would call *'le jeu du monde'*?

JB: That comes close to it. The Heraclitean inspiration is identical. The play of forms is where the elements are all in collusion, but at the same time hostile to each other, as with water and fire. Forms play on an endless circularity. Forms involve a game, a set of rules, and rituals. I believe this kind of progression, this devolution one to another – though without passing through meaning, individuation and difference – still exists. I believe we are always playing. This passion for the play of forms persists, but we resist it by psychological *mise en scène*, by the play of affects and desire. You then get into insoluble contradictions in which subjects function in terms of their reciprocal difference. To this energy differential, with its too-human origins, I prefer an energy which comes from elsewhere.

PP: Can you give us other examples of these forms?

JB: Language is always a possible example. It's important because it lies on the rift between the human and inhuman worlds. Language is both what cuts us off from global circulation – of the animal and plant kingdoms, and so on – but at the same time it's what restores that symbolic circulation. Fundamentally, it's through the use of language that we get back not to an instinctual animality, but to a radicalness of forms. Language, while belonging to the domain of illusion, allows us to play with that illusion. Through it, we enter into a complicity with the world that has nothing to do with the mastery of meaning. Language remains a kind of miracle in that it separates us from the world, while keeping the illusion of the world safe and sound.

It's more difficult to point to examples in more worldly areas. But even in our daily existences, carried on under the sway of the economy, of considerations of psychology and energy, another kind of relationship, which is at the same time arbitrary and random, is in play, and establishes a form of convention that's both lower-order, imperceptible, unconscious and higher-order, charged with complicity. There's a dimension of play, including in those areas where everything seems to function according to laws. There's a secret rule. You can't lay it bare. You can't stage its operation. You can't play by both the law and the rule at the same time. I'm secretly convinced that people don't see themselves as individuals, that they're not what they are, and live in the form of play. Without this kind of drift, this exchange, this unconscious otherness, things would be unbearable. If one lived only in differential relationships, the relation of the will and representation, the world itself would not survive.

PP: What makes you say that we're in a relation of forms today, not a relation of forces?

JB: We aren't. I just think that the exhaustion of relations of forces, and of the value systems that go with them, creates a different, original situation. There are periods and cultures where this kind of play comes to the surface. In primitive cultures (without going back nostalgically to positions which were those of *Symbolic Exchange*), this play of forms is the rule. Similarly, art has kept alive the possibility of playing out this illusion to the full and finding the rules for it, to the exclusion of any reality. Genuine art doesn't concern itself with the question of the real or its law. These are configurations which find their own response in accordance with their own rules.

PP: Isn't all this, in spite of everything, burdened with historicity? Isn't there a hidden teleology to your pattern of thought?

JB: I don't ask myself that question. It's possible that in my medulla, there's also a millenarian dimension to all this! I'd have no objection to that. You don't escape your own culture.

PP: The psychical space isn't your cup of tea, is it?

JB: Not really. People first have a destiny, then a history. The two don't necessarily overlap. Some will live their whole lives solely in the historical, everyday, individual dimension, in the sense that they'll be able to tell themselves their histories, refer to what they've been through, seek out their origins. Others will live without any story about themselves, and live out their destinies without history. Individuality and personality are so many weak concepts. What constitutes an event in life is a conjunction between the world as it is and the play of the world, in which the best and the worst are always in play: the event from elsewhere. It happens to you even before you've willed it. The will is always retrospective. It comes to sanction something that has already taken place. It's like plans: you do something, and retrospectively, you conceive the plan. It's like the reconstructing of the dream text at the moment of waking. The will is there to put a final stamp on what has taken place in another way. Psychoanalysis has spoken a certain number of truths on this, but it has locked the subject up in its psychical, relational space.

PP: Aren't you perhaps something of a Gnostic?

JB: I wouldn't have minded being Manichaean, heretical and Gnostic. Why not? But I've never ventured to draw up a list of secret references. What would be the good of disclosing them?

PP: Reconstituting the forms of destiny can quite simply mean doing the history of ideas, in the noble manner of Sir Isaiah Berlin, in the great humanist tradition. Isn't there within you a secret resolve not to give in to this kind of genealogical thinking, either in this humanist form or in the epistemic form, as attempted by Michel Foucault on the clinical institution and prison? How is it that, since *Symbolic Exchange and Death*, you're averse to genealogy?

JB: It's my way of opting for a 'fatal strategy' of thought. That is to say, for thought not caught up in the history of ideas or in a philosophical itinerary but, rather, in the current situation as final term. Treating every situation, every moment of present events, as though it were the last. The diagonal between the fatal and the event. What in the event is done against history, is irreducible to history. What in thought is irreducible to the reason of the subject, what in the object is irreducible to the subject. Ultimately, I am after irreducibles.

PP: Would you accept the term viral thought?

JB: Viral . . . yes. In the sense that thought creates chain reactions. In that sense, yes, there is a virality or virulence. On the other hand, virality is part of the world of contagion. It's absolute promiscuity, and hence precisely the opposite of the succession of forms. Virality's a very mysterious phenomenon. There's a mode of action and propagation which is no longer a form, which is of the order of the formless and is, at the same time, an extreme phenomenon of prodigious effectiveness. Why is that being discovered today? How is it that virality, which previously – at least in the thought and action of men – quite simply didn't exist, suddenly does now? We don't know what viruses are about, what their purpose is, if they have one. It's doubtless because they don't have one that they're so disturbingly effective. The irruption of this indeterminate causality throws everything into question. As a result, thought, too, has to become viral. For better or for worse.

PP: Might we say of viruses that they have a fatal strategy?

JB: The fatal strategy is often understood as the catastrophic development internal to the system. For me, it meant precisely the opposite. It meant finding a form of play and destiny which precisely thwarted that implacable development of the system. For that development isn't fatal at all, but banal. The fatal strategy was the reinvention of a thought which explodes not the truth of the system, but its logic. Against the strategy of evil, that of the greater evil.

PP: Aren't you simply trying to reinject destiny into our societies?

JB: I don't want to stress destiny or the fatal too much. There's been too much confusion about this. Only the play of destiny is interesting, but it isn't a religious fate we're talking about. It means simply that, as against cause-and-effect logic, the event is there first. Any form of interpretation or explanation is of the order of repentance. This is akin to the meaning of character for Nietzsche. More than in politics or anatomy, destiny is registered in character. It's our specific sign. It's a bit like modern physics, where each object invents its own space, its own time. It's destined for itself. It creates its own destiny. It has its character. It has its specific, implacable sign which means that it's always faced with the same ultimate fate. This doesn't exclude having a history. Destiny and history are two parallel dimensions. They don't meet, save in exceptional and dramatic situations. The mistake is to confuse the two, as psychoanalysis and the human sciences too often do.

PP: I'm struck by your constancy. Following your intellectual itinerary since *The Consumer Society* in 1970, one gets the impression that the social destiny of the contemporary individual is foreclosed. From personalization conceived as lowest marginal difference in the 1970 book to the ready-made, cloned individual of 1995, there's no last chance for postmodern man. Or rather, there is one, but outside the social field and its determinations. How can you both condemn the individual to become a ready-made, and at the same time maintain that playing with his destiny is all he has left?

JB: I don't 'condemn' the individual, and I don't reduce destiny to 'all we have left'. I maintain one thesis against another. The ready-made individual is an ultra-modern product. This isn't the concept of the bourgeois individual, but the concept of postmodernity. It isn't a subject; it's become a kind of clone. It has a strange status; it's like a particle, a corpuscle, a molecule, a free electron, a monad. This individual is no longer subject to a destiny. He has in a sense exchanged his destiny for a fateful [*fatal*] experimentation on himself. I think of all those dangerous adventures, those almost sacrificial, mutilatory bodily ordeals. Take the disabled athletes of Atlanta who mutilated themselves to improve their performances. This means that the individual is forced to create a sort of adversity artificially to stand in for a destiny. He is, in fact, caught in his own trap. He doesn't play with anything any longer; he tests, he experiments – which is the opposite of play. He deliberately goes looking for all the risks which nature and destiny would previously have exposed him to. He'd have fought to survive. Today he's forced artificially to re-create the conditions of survival. It's staggering to see this invention of artificial risks. Extending even as far as one's own body, with genetic experimentation. All done in order to maintain at the very least the fiction of an otherness, an other. But it's no longer the otherness of seduction, it's the artificial alterity of an otherness laboratory, of a *trompe-l'œil* destiny. Are we all trapped in this simulated adversity? The weakening of destiny, the lack of destiny, is our big issue. In an ultra-protected, ultra-integrated world, where the risks are part of the great recycling, the individual is desperately seeking an identity. The worst of it is that the individual's only recourse is to pit himself against that ultimate value of identity which, in my opinion, isn't a value, or is at least a weak value in which everyone finds himself confronted by the crucial problem: what am I? What do I want? Where is the other? He becomes once again an individual grappling with his shadow, or one who has lost that shadow once and for all.

PP: What, then, would be your conception of that real philosophical monster, identity?

JB: Identity is a dream pathetic in its absurdity. You dream of being yourself when you've nothing better to do. You dream of that when you've lost all singularity (and culture is precisely the extreme form of singularity of a society). Today, sadly, we no longer fight for sovereignty or glory, we fight for identity. Sovereignty was a mastery; identity is merely a reference. Sovereignty was adventurous; identity is linked to security (and, unfortunately, also to the security and control systems which impose identity on you). Identity is this obsession with recognition of the liberated being, but liberated in a vacuum, and with no idea at all now where he is. It's an existence label. All energies − of peoples, entire minorities and individuals − are concentrated today on this derisory affirmation, this statement bereft of pride: I am! I exist! I'm alive, I'm called so-and-so, I'm European! You have to prove the obvious and, having done so, suddenly it's not obvious at all.

Identity is an insoluble problem. For better or for worse, it's the desperate fantasy of the whole technical, rational enterprise. The aim is, indeed, to identify everything by excluding the negative aspect, by excluding evil and producing self-identical molecular beings. Identification of the individual, the subject, the nation, the race − identification of the very world itself, now technically and absolutely real – having become what it is, and that's all there is to it. So there's no longer any possibility of metaphor, of metamorphosis – only the indefinite metastasis of identity remains.

The mirror-stage has given way to the video-stage. Nothing escapes this kind of image-recording, sound-recording, this immediate, simultaneous consciousness-recording, any more. Nothing takes place now without a screen. It's not a mirror any more. Living identity, the identity of the subject, implied the mirror, the element of reflection. Even in the shattered mirror of alienation, the Student of Prague rediscovered his image on the verge of death. We no longer have such good fortune. What we get now isn't really our own image, but an instantaneous recording in real time. In real time, there isn't even the distance of an image. But, merely to exist, you need distance from yourself. The abolition of that distance condemns us to indefinite reproduction, to a kind of derisory immortality which no longer has anything in common with the immortality of destiny. I would say the same of 'liberation'. Hasn't liberation, in all its forms, been both the accomplishment of, and the final blow to, liberty? This is the whole problem of modernity.

The whole movement of modernity, its negative destiny, lies in the fact of transcribing all that was of the order of the imaginary, the dream, the ideal and utopia into technical and operational reality. It was a radical disalienation, then, this materialization of all desires, this hyperrealization of all possibilities. Unconditional accomplishment. No otherness, impossibility or transcendence in which to take refuge any more. No more alienated people: an individual who is totally fulfilled – virtually, of course. It's the virtual dimension which monopolizes all the other worlds today, which totalizes the real by evacuating any imaginary alternative. It's from the point when it no longer has the imaginary to carry it on, and lapses into the virtual, that the real is truly dead. The individual finally becomes identical with himself – the promise of the Self (the 'I') has been realized. The prophecy which was that of the whole of modern history, that of Hegel, Marx, Stirner, the Situationists – the prophecy of the end of the separated subject – has come to pass. But it has come to pass not for better, but for worse: from the Other to the same, from alienation to identification (just as the Nietzschean prophecy of the trans-valuation of values has come to pass for the worse in the movement not beyond, but this side of, good and evil).

PP: For you, the individual, as Gilles Deleuze said, is immediately collective. You're still a Nietzschean in this. You still make no distinction between what is individual and what is collective. . . .

JB: That distinction is of the order of moral philosophy. A whole history of the subject and the individual has developed, in opposition to the social. But today that subject has fallen under a spell. It's lost its freedom, it's no longer master of its origins or its ends, it's the hostage of the network. Priority is with the network, not with the subscribers to the network. Identity is on the network's side, not on that of the individual. The collective, too, takes the form of the network. Virtual hyperreality has swallowed both terms together. The individual/collective polarities are fading.

PP: What, then, can constitute an event for the individual?

JB: His singularity. Not individuality, and not collectivity either, because this has become the globalism of the network in which the individual is now merely a particle. On the other hand, singularity might be said to be what constitutes an event. A singularity that's no longer individual, nor the creation of a determinate subject, but the product of a bursting-in, a breaking-in. It can come from a person, a group, an accident in the system itself. It's an anomaly which acquires its force within the indistinct ensemble of the system.

The individual in the system is residual, whereas the singularity is antagonistic. The singularity has a total autonomy, and exists only as such. The system is destroyed in spite of itself, whereas the singularity has the privilege of destroying itself. Everyone plays out their disappearance, but the singularity plays it out itself, in control of the rules of the game. The singularity is made for a very rapid disappearance. But that isn't a catastrophic fatality. Appearance and disappearance are the form of destiny.

Chapter 4
Present Considerations

Philippe Petit: Does the transpolitical which you evoke mean the end of the political? Reading you, one has the sense that the political space is undefinable, that political action is something improbable. Don't you think the Right of all Rights – namely the fundamental rights of the human person, otherwise known as human rights – could fill this gap in politics, and open up a path to new actions? I'm thinking of the way the notion of the crime against humanity has now entered positive law under pressure from jurists and from citizens who've been the victims of all kinds of exactions. For example, when intellectuals protest to governments that the Hague Tribunal's arrest warrants aren't being carried out, aren't they doing their duty?

Jean Baudrillard: It's possible to see things quite differently. Far from attesting to an advance in the international moral conscience, the very fact of the Hague Tribunal being held is the expression of the impotence of Western nations to intervene effectively on the ground, their moral and political incapacity to enforce the law: that impotence is turned into a tribunal (let us leave aside the hypothesis that such impotence is not innocent, and that it corresponds to a more or less deliberate strategy, merely coupled with guilty conscience and bad faith: the tribunal is also the expression of all that).

As for the intellectuals' petition, it's the mark, in its turn, of the total impotence of the Hague Tribunal to have its decisions obeyed. There again, one may doubt the real resolve to translate law into reality. Moreover, this creates a peculiar situation in which law progresses on its own account, without any real consequences, and perhaps even providing cover as it does so for an aggravation of the real situation. Ultimately, the law is laid down merely to be transgressed – it becomes the perfect alibi for the perfect crime. The appearance of moral progress merely attests to actual impotence and, in this sense, is complicit with it. So it's absurd to sign a petition which sanctions the complicit, and perhaps calculated, impotence of the 'responsible' powers. And, indeed, there's something ridiculous in prostituting oneself for no hope of gain, since it has become blindingly obvious that the power concerned either simply doesn't exist or has taken the decision not to exert itself. Now, what is a power without political will?

One can say, then, that if the Western powers have fully taken on the dishonour of the situation, the intellectuals, for their part, have taken on the ridicule. In these conditions, not signing, far from being indifference or contempt, is a positive act in relation to the general collusion, from top to bottom of the scale, in accrediting and endorsing the massacre. The idea that the universal extension of law is progress is too good to be true. No other progress of consciousness has ever been detected than that of bad conscience, parallel to the progress of bad faith, the two being merged in the general rise of *ressentiment*, understood as the latest stage in the genealogy of morals.

PP: In what sense does that condemn law to merely marking time? After 1945, in spite of the impact of war, jurists like René Cassin invented new juridical projects. Why shouldn't that be possible at the end of this century?

JB: There isn't any unilateral progress of law, either. What we're seeing is a simultaneous and contradictory recrudescence of law and denial of justice. The Hague condemns the war criminals, and the UN military conspicuously declare that they won't arrest them. The judges carry out a search at Tiberi's flat and the police, clearly under orders from the government, conspicuously oppose the judicial procedure.[9] Not to mention the Algerian elections (isn't universal suffrage progress?) – free elections immediately suppressed by a military *coup d'état* with the assent of the 'democratic' powers. How do things stand with law, then? How do things stand with an international tribunal, contested by the very forces of the highest international authority, which is already objectively complicit in ethnic cleansing on the ground, and here openly guilty of a denial of justice? Human rights, inscribed above the portals of all the democracies, are what get given to those who have landed up on the wrong side of the universal.

PP: And French intellectuals? Would you say that they, too, have landed up on the wrong side of the universal?

JB: French intellectuals cultivate the same fiction of their universal influence as do French leaders of their global political power. The same French self-delusion and complacency. And at the domestic level, there's the same pretension on the part of the intellectuals to influence national political decisions as our leaders have of influencing international politics. The intellectuals (those who assert themselves as such and, at the same time, as a moral conscience) are always fussing around, putting their oar in, in spite of massive historical evidence on the flagrant pointlessness of doing so, as benevolent advisers to a government which – and this is the most grotesque element – no longer really is one. For there to be a counsellor to the Prince, there has to be a Prince. And that non-government itself seeks to interfere in world politics to influence events when it doesn't have the means to do so and, in any case, even those who seem to decide world politics (the White House, for example) are only ever the operators, or clones, of a multinational machinery recast by Bill Gates, the banks and international speculation – all of which now function in almost total autonomy, following quasi-automatic strategies. And all this in the void: this is the last irony of history which no one seems aware of, so impatient are they all to have their role in that history. From one rung of the ladder to another, everyone imagines they are manipulating on their own account, everyone ruinously conforms to a crazy scenography in an aimless spiral (but do spirals ever have an aim?), in which all are complicit without knowing it.

PP: In what way does this irony of history prevent us from imagining a beyond of capitalism?

JB: But who or what would take us beyond (if not the system itself)? In the old historical relation, there's an antagonistic polarity, not a collusive one. There are oppressed and oppressors. And the oppressed don't live in recrimination; they live in revolt. Today, everyone is locked up in their victim's claims. So there's no revolt any more, no antagonism, but a perverse situation, a new perverse, consensual social contract in which everyone tries to gain their recognition as a victim. Everyone becomes both victim and accomplice in this. Everyone is on both sides of the fracture – if, indeed, there is a fracture. At any rate, it's no longer a line marking a conflict or a relation of forces but, rather, an involutive line, the line of an unhealthy complicity with the state of things.

Take the example of Crédit Lyonnais. The taxpayers are going to have to pay 180 billion francs to bail out Crédit Lyonnais. In the past, it was the state which did the bailing out – which, admittedly, amounted to the same thing – but now the responsibility is clearly assigned: capital, confident in its impunity, can step forward without its mask, saying explicitly: 'Capital is you! The State is you!' Moreover, the Crédit Lyonnais affair is just another extension of social provision and welfare. If all cases of social need are taken care of, there's no reason not to assist Crédit Lyonnais when it's in distress. By contrast, the unemployed and the various cases for social assistance are now given to understand that they have to look after themselves, that they have to manage their 'enterprise' better. The individual is treated as a capitalist business, and the capitalist business as a citizen on welfare. The role-reversal is perfect – the social has backfired in a manner entirely to the advantage of capital.

The system has become a Moebius strip, where everyone is both victim of, and party to, the crime. If Crédit Lyonnais falls, you fall. If the factory closes, you clear out! So, Crédit Lyonnais is you! The company is you! This wasn't true in the classic age of capital and exploitation, when the demarcation line between oppressed and oppressors, exploited and exploiters, was clear. The same forced complicity and collusion, and hence the same blackmail, takes place in the political sphere. '*L'État, c'est moi! L'État, c'est nous!*' has subtly become '*L'État, c'est vous!*' What a democratic marvel it is, this transference of responsibility! The citizen is now a shareholder; he no longer has any interest in seeing the business go under. And consequently, Revolution, in which those at the bottom took power, has given way to Devolution, in which the government itself cedes its powers from the top down. Democratic trickery or the ruse of history? The fact is that this transfer of responsibility corresponds to a diabolic twisting of the democratic principle: it's capital connecting back to itself like a Leyden jar, or curling into a spiral. But is it still capital? 'Don't ask what the State can do for you, ask what you can do for the State.' The perfect formula for interactivity as a strategy for calling the population to order, for transferring all problems on to those on the receiving end. Parody of the ideal of the reappropriation of one's own destiny.

PP: It's also the parody of political emancipation. Is capitalism for you the cold monster Simone Weil referred to when speaking of the State?

JB: It's a monster which is standing social liberation on its head. It's capital now that's emancipating itself from the workers! It's parents who are liberating themselves from their children! End of the Oedipus complex, end of the class struggle, in whose shade everything worked so well. All the flows are being reversed. The talk was all of freedom, of emancipation, of transforming as much fatality as possible into liberty. Today, it's evident that the great wave of liberation is simply the best way of giving the slaves back a bogus power and freedom.

Forced interaction: the masses now intervene directly in the event through the ratings and all the other immediate feedback devices: they've become interactive! And in opinion polls we're all involved statistically: forced complicity. In any case, we've been interactive for a long time, like it or not, through all the automatic response systems we're enslaved to. And the interactivity we're being offered will never – by a long chalk – be the equal of the interactivity we already suffer: the collective interpassivity which the other form merely prolongs with information and communications technologies.

This is why it's impossible, in the interactive sphere, to raise the problem of freedom and responsibility. People are almost amazed that they have children (are children ever amazed that they have parents?). They're amazed at being responsible for them, as at many other things. They're amazed at having to take charge of their own lives. They haven't the heart for it any more; they've no convictions. In present conditions, they're even amazed at having a body. There's no longer any real basis for all that. It no longer imposes itself on the imagination or on consciousness as a value, nor even on the unconscious as a fantasy. In this context, any responsibility or appeal to responsibility is surrealistic. They might just as well be amazed at having to seek work – as they might at being relay stations for lots of meaningless networks, the involuntary actors in a general interactive comedy – the targets for demands and questions for which they are merely the automatic answering machines.

PP: Are they amazed, at least, that they live in silent collusion with the powers that be?

JB: Not even that, since they're in collusion with a power which, strictly speaking, no longer even exists, which is even worse. Which is simultaneously invested and disinvested by everyone, like a revolving stage or a zero-sum variable geometry. Everyone plays along in the comedy of power (as in many others besides: the comedy of the social or of culture). But I retain the hope that there's a double game going on here, both individual and collective. One ought to be able to prevent this situation from perpetuating itself, to disconnect it, break down the consensual sequence. But one can hardly have any illusions, either about the awareness generated or about revolt following. In a history in progress, you create an event if you anticipate, if you create more rapid conditions of development, and hence an explosive differential. In an involutive curve like ours, by attempting to speed up or correct the system you contribute to the involution. We're trapped. We're part of the automatic writing of the system. But there are unconscious forms of social upheaval and creeping revolt against this forced participation we've been speaking of. For example, there has gradually emerged recently into popular consciousness (unconsciousness) the (old, '68) idea that consumption is a con.

PP: The consumer has supplanted the citizen, then. Hence, as you noted in your book of 1970,[10] the intense guilt which attaches to this new style of hedonistic behaviour.

JB: Even in the reptilian brain of the grass-roots consumer, it's become clear, when faced with power's economic ultimatum – consume, consume, or the machine will grind to a halt – that consumers have become hostages, guinea pigs. After the general mobilization of the worker, then the soldier, then the citizen in universal suffrage (vote any way you like, but vote!), we now have the mobilization of the consumer. And, with it, new latent forms of resistance when those from whom one wishes to extort need, expenditure as a social obligation – having extorted speech, votes, sex and happiness from them – realize what 'embolic' power they have in relation to the system: quite simply to consume less – not out of conscientious objection, or even from political resolve, but as a self-defence reflex.

Here again, an agonizing revision of the watchwords of modernity is in prospect – the watchwords of growth and welfare. It's a revisionism, this refusal to consume, a social treason in the eyes of the dominant free-market liberalism. A new class struggle is beginning (if the herd doesn't want to graze, how is one to make one's butter?).

PP: There is perhaps a new political economy to bring about. Reversibility can also take the form of the re-founding of the economic sphere. I'm thinking of the contaminated blood affair, mad cows, asbestos. . . .

JB: Is this still political economy? I think the two terms, the economic and the political, have mingled their determinations and, so to speak, imploded into one another. We're in the postscript of a history or a political economy in which we're dealing with the waste products of two centuries of capital and production, including human waste. For thirty years or more we've been engaged in the management of waste, in a politics and an economy of dejection – which clearly involves a certain abjection – in an interminable enterprise of recycling, cleansing and laundering, and this, once again, includes human material. And not only in its social dimension, but in the reprocessing of the genetic capital of the species. The whole system of modernity has embarked upon repentance and assumed a victim's perspective, as though we were dealing with a historical catastrophe of the human race that already existed, had already occurred, and the recycling of that catastrophe. We're all impersonal victims of this virtual catastrophe, this backfiring of capital and history, from which we re-emerge as its symptoms and its multiple waste products. Hence the agonizing revision of modernity in which we're engaged, excluded from ourselves by the unconditional liberation of all our desires. In this sense, we're in a fundamentally revisionist society.

The whole century is currently in mourning for, and repenting, all the liberations it has desired and accommodated, all the bounds it has burst – everything it was enslaved to and is now orphaned by. All the gains of modernity and liberation in recession – sex, tobacco, alcohol, speed, abortions: activities which are now clandestine, doomed to prohibition and apartheid, refused a residence permit or cloistered in reserves. A general revisionist movement and a tide now flowing the other way – for future generations, this will all doubtless form part of what they never knew (happiness or hell!). For us, at least, those things still had the time to exist. But with the precession of the prohibition, they will disappear from circulation without even having appeared. Similarly, with all the ideals of modernity, the ideals of the Enlightenment, of happiness, well-being and freedom, their technical realization amounts to a violent desublimation. All that was liberated is currently being liquidated.

PP: Can't one, then, liberate oneself from liberation?

JB: The paradox of liberation is that the people liberated are never the ones you think: children, slaves, women or colonial peoples. It's always the others liberating themselves *from them*, getting rid of them in the name of a principle of freedom and emancipation. Hence the dramatic concern of children to ensure that parents don't stop being parents, or at least that they do so as late as possible. Hence the collective concern to beg the State not to stop being the State, to force it to take on its role, whereas it's constantly trying to relinquish that role – and with good reason. The State is constantly 'liberating' the citizens, urging them to look after themselves – something they generally don't want to do at all. In this sense, we're all potential Bartlebys: 'I would prefer not to'. Be free! Be responsible! Take responsibility for yourself! – 'I would prefer not to'. Preferring not to, rather than willing something (Philippe Lançon, *Libération*). Preferring not to any more. Not to run any more, or compete, or consume, and not, at any price, to be free. This is all part of the pattern of a repentance of modernity, of a subtle indifference which senses the dangers of a responsibility and an emancipation which are too good to be true. Hence the currently triumphant sentimental, familial, political and moral revisionism, which can take on the more violent aspect of a 'reactionary' hatred of oneself or others, the product of the disillusionment that follows liberatory violence. This opposite tide, this 'regressive' resublimation, is the contemporary form – and, so to speak, the consequence – of the repressive desublimation analysed by Marcuse. Decidedly, freedom isn't simple, and liberation even less so.

However, as the orgy of modernity, the orgy of liberation, is clearly ambivalent, containing within it both the best and the worst, the agonizing revision of that modernity, of its ideals and its illusions, is necessarily ambivalent too. So, all the freedoms acquired are gradually being suspended or 'overhauled', market freedom compensating for the loss of all the others. But the end of sexual liberation (in behaviour, if not *de jure*) can be evaluated in various ways, with some 'reactionary' aspects appearing downright positive. People seem, for example, to have got over the total freedom to consume and spend. They seem to have sensed the trap in that. What we have, rather, is a new savings campaign (of retraction and disinvestment in all its forms), and it has changed meaning. Whereas once it was conservative and antimodern in relation to the general dynamism, thrift is now the weapon of a movement of recalcitrant small savers. The consumption strike: last resistance to enforced free circulation. Since they can't withdraw themselves from free circulation, they withdraw their money, retract a part of their needs. Massive resistance to the oiling of the wheels; instinctive regulation, revolt against forced deregulation (we are all force-fed geese; animals, by contrast, never eat too much). And if people no longer wish to consume? And if they no longer want to be 'free'? This is all reactionary, politically incorrect. One can clearly see that the revision of the imperatives of modernity is ambiguous, and sometimes subtly revolutionary. The end of modernity is precisely the point at which all the effects of progress, growth and liberation become ambivalent. That's when the Left and democracy lose the plot, and where each apparent advance (including advances in freedom and human rights) has to be assessed *sub specie ambiguitatis* and *a contrario*.

PP: What form does that revision of modernity's imperatives take, as you see it?

JB: This agonizing revisionism is clearly taking a necrological form. We've been in a 'necro' phase since the 1980s. 'Necro' of socialism grappling with its own corpse and the corpse of history. Mitterrandian 'necro', with a ghost president vampirizing a decalcified society. Death throes of the grand narratives and all the ideals of modernity. A holocaust in just a few years of a whole generation of intellectual big names (Sartre, Barthes, Lacan, Foucault, Althusser, Deleuze, Debord). Countless episodes of commemorative necrophagy ('68, the French Revolution, Rimbaud, Nietzsche, Van Gogh, to name but a few – not to mention the Heidegger affair and all the necroactive convulsions linked to the Holocaust and the war). We've seen the fall of the Wall and the end of communism, but an unresolved work of mourning, inasmuch as on this occasion we no longer have the spectre of communism haunting Europe, but the defunct spectre of communism haunting the end of history – perhaps it'll haunt it more effectively dead than alive?

PP: Is this what you call generalized repetition?

JB: To the universal 'necro' must clearly be added the universal beatification, *in vitro* or *in vivo*, of those who remain or survive, in the spectral shade of the Pope in his persistent vegetative state.

Repentance is part of this necrological, revisionist turnabout. It's one of the essential engines of our public and political life today. The Courtier was the most remarkable figure of the aristocratic order. The Militant was the most remarkable figure of the social and revolutionary order. The Penitent is the most remarkable figure of the advanced democratic order. be But don't worry: one can be both a courtier and a penitent, a militant and a penitent, a militant and a courtier (they are the worst). Perhaps we are all penitents. Repentance has passed from the sphere of eighties Italian Leftism to the whole of the political class, and today it has become a principle of government (including the form of forced repentance that is the hunt for corruption scandals) or, at any rate, a principle of success and prestige. One has only to look at men like F.F. or R.D., among so many others, who have in their time profited in all possible ways from collusion with the powerful (whether communist or Mitterrandian), only to take the payoff ('with bonuses') twenty years after from the disappearance of that same power. Yet repentance, apart from showing a *ressentiment* towards one's own cause, and adding dishonestly to denial, is unjustifiable: it attests to a misconception of history and modernity itself, since it accords these things the status of unconditional revelation, only to run them down and do a negative 'rewrite' on the scenario as soon as they have failed. This is to back a loser at both ends of the process, and there is an implacable bad faith of all penitents (those repenting of socialism, of modernity, of the politically correct) in wearyingly playing out their destinies as victims, fascinated by their failure and licking their own wounds to infect them, while deriving the secondary gains from the situation.

PP: Does this repentance condemn the political class to a walk-on part?

JB: The State and political power sit atop all this in a very, very fragile position; they are, so to speak, like filigree-work upon a translucent society, like a fiction woven from multiple complicities. They allow themselves to be regenerated by all who combat them. The political class gets itself investigated and regenerated by the examining magistrates. It's as though there were a strategy here (the government putting itself in the position of victim), but in fact there isn't any political will at the top any longer. There's merely an internal perversion, an internal convolution of the system, which means that one can no longer be in an oppositional position. There is, then, a dangerous pretension on the part of the government to govern when it hasn't either the means or the will to do so any longer; but there's an even more deceitful and dangerous pretension among those who think they can reverse or overthrow the system, for even if they have the will to do so, they do precisely the opposite of what they intended. Now, the worst thing today is the lack of lucidity. When you're in a trap, you're in a trap. There's no point fighting on a terrain where the models for neutralizing opposition are strongest, where you're up against the spiralling trap of a system that is master both of the positive and of the negative. In that case, you mustn't look to some internal negativity any longer. You have to look either to the achievement, by saturation and concentration – by the system's excess of positivity – of a critical mass, and then it's no longer the negative but the more-positive-than-positive that produces the upheaval; or to singularities, perfectly anomalous objects or events, which are neither inside nor outside. It's in this twisting of the system, in its automatic recycling by the negative, its absorption of all dysfunctions, that the essence of corruption and the baneful destiny of democracy lie.

PP: Listening to you, that destiny seems inescapable. It's no use asking what you think of those who are intent on refounding democratic citizenship.

JB: At the current time, democracy is a social form that's about as ancestral as the symbolic exchange of primitive societies. And we dream of it in the same way. The political in general continues to be the waking dream of Western societies – of the exoteric societies where everything is expressed by technics. The esoteric societies, for their part (whether they are disinherited or traditional societies), long since brought politics into line with tribal arrangements. They have trapped and tamed the Western machinery of politics, law, democracy and the universal in their personal structures and relations; they have integrated linearity and history into their own cycle. We may ask ourselves whether, on a much vaster scale and by the roundabout route of rationality, it isn't the same with our Western societies. Doesn't the political sphere obey impulses, obligations, challenges and fantasies that have little to do with public affairs? This incorruptible truth of evil, of the irrational, shows through in the very corruption of the political, which must therefore be interpreted positively as the impossibility of Political Reason realizing itself. This is what explains why the more imperative transparency becomes, the greater the corruption. By wishing merely to take into account a politically correct human nature – a fundamentally Rousseauist vision – the militants of the good democratic cause – those who, more subtly, wish to rehabilitate the 'essence' of the political – merely feed this corrupt form of the social. What is the point of setting a purpose for an enlightened dimension of the political and the social spheres, when it's becoming increasingly obvious, most particularly in the economic sphere, that these things are caught up with much stranger purposes, if not indeed with no purpose at all? There's a kind of savage delusion and – not to put too fine a point on it – stupidity, in stubbornly pressing on in the right direction when there is no direction, in wishing to change the form of the equation when it's equal to zero.

Just look at all the battles everywhere on corrupt fronts: in the electoral system, where people are led to fight for equivalent castes; in the employment field, where everyone has to fight to find a place in a system of exploitation, a relatively favoured spot in a labour market which simultaneously serves the government as a blackmailing technique. Everywhere we're trapped in false problems, false alternatives, false issues, in which we lose out come what may.

PP: So here we are, under democratic house arrest! All right. But what intrigues me is that your lack of political hope is accompanied by a thinking on violence in the style of Sorel, a thinking which is, to say the least, pessimistic. On this question, you're quite close to Yves Michaud, though you don't in fact come to the same conclusions.[11] I can't manage to dispel a certain ambiguity where your conception of violence is concerned. One can't tell whether you see it as a rudimentary, archaic instrument of action, as Michaud does, or whether you maintain a certain fascination for it. Once again, you sometimes put me in mind of Cioran, a right-wing intellectual if ever there was one, who regarded democracy as a regime which prohibited anger and revolution. So, when you state that our society leaves no room for 'real violence', is this said with regret or satisfaction?

JB: It's a diagnosis. Our society has expelled violence (at the same time as it has expelled evil, illness, negativity and death – I don't mean it has eliminated them, but it has expelled them from its system of values). All forms of wildcat, spontaneous violence, historical and political, have been stifled or neutralized. Just as all forms of concrete freedom are being absorbed into the only freedom which remains, the freedom of the market and of market values, and the assumption of these into globalism, so all forms of violence are reduced and muzzled to the exclusive advantage of the terrorist and police-style violence of the new world order. The system has the monopoly of violence: a monopoly of the extermination of any singularity, any negativity, of death itself, and of real violence in the virtual violence of generalized pacification, fundamentalist [*intégriste*] violence (the only violence, that of the system, not that of terrorists, which remains small-scale and blind).

Against this, new forms of violence are arising; or, rather, new forms of anonymous, anomalous virulence – a reactive, reactional vehemence against the dominant thrust of society, against any dominant system – which is no longer a historical violence of liberation, but a violence from the confines of a sacrificed destiny, from the confines of a sacrificed symbolic order, from the confines of the perfect crime or, in other words, of total integration (the integrism of the system) and even of the democratic aspects of the system (enforced liberation, enforced interactivity in all its forms) – that is to say, the absence of destiny. This new violence is no longer directed against the absence of freedom and against oppression, but against the absence of destiny and the democratic leukaemia of all our cells.

PP: An absence like that exhibited by H.B., the hostage-taker at the Neuilly infants' school in 1995. In a book which – sadly – passed unnoticed, Alain Brossat wrote of him:

> What the public will not forgive the 'monster' is his directly exhibiting . . . what is basi-cally at stake in the crisis: not the economy, but living beings, not objects, but human relations, not car sales figures, but whether or not the lifeworld is fit to live in. . . .[12]

JB: He's right, because that violence on the part of H.B. or Florence Rey[13] is no longer a political violence with a determinate objective (political violence has been absorbed and transformed into transpolitical energy for the benefit of the system). It's a violence cut off from its object and turning back against that object itself – against the political and the social. It's no longer anarchistic or revolution-ary, it's worse, because its objective is no longer to set the system to rights or to transform the world by violently and historically bringing something new into being; it takes the system itself as its object, aiming at systematic destabilization. It's not interested in the system's internal contradictions; it targets the very principle of the social and the political. It spontaneously takes a viral, temperamental form. It's an esoteric form which is its own justification, an exclusive violence which is merely the correlative of a system of exclusion. It answers the systematic exclusion our society practises by even more exclusion, cutting itself off from the social world by indifference or hatred. For it may be aggravated or apathetic: it may take the form of an active terrorism or that of the inertia and irrepressible conformism of the masses.

No longer having either object or objective, it wilfully (like all forms of virus and virulence) confuses the murderer and the victim, in an immense Stockholm syndrome, precisely reflecting in this the system itself and its 'perfect crime' – that is to say, its current ideal operation in which we are all simultaneously victims, murderers and accomplices (this is the truth of consensus, interactivity, and everything cycling back on itself). Taking a lofty, otherworldly view of the whole process – the process of the system and that of the violence which opposes it while reflecting its characteristic features (exclusion, autarky, anomaly, virulence) – one might conclude that it's an immense suicidal process, suicide being the perfect crime, inasmuch as in that act murderer and victim are one.

In the history of humanity, then, the various lethal forms of violence are coming increasingly to resemble one another, as the terms are mingled and the roles merged (a confusion opened up irreversibly by the nuclear and by all the forms of complicity in pollution and death) to the point of wiping out, in the logical functioning of the system, any demarcation line between accomplice and victim (as any demarcation line between subject and object is being wiped out in philosophy and the sciences), and giving the image of a collective suicide, in which the attribution of responsibility becomes entirely secondary.

PP: But the threshold you speak of at which we break with this can, it seems, have only a clandestine existence. How are we to go on living in your world, our world, without being compromised?

JB: The only exception is singularity. Singularity is the singularity of that anomalous violence I'm referring to, the singularity which stands opposed to real violence, to the violence of any reality principle. For the basic violence, the basic deception, is the violence of the reality principle. Now, the system produces more and more reality, more and more of the social, more and more politics, more and more sex, more and more information, etc. That is its own peculiar violence. But at the same time, and in the same process, it paradoxically produces more and more singularity (of beings, of unidentified, refractory, excluded forces, which have no need of it to exist and are definitively exiled from the system). The example of the social sphere is fantastic. One day soon, that sphere will be fully realized, and the only people remaining will be the 'excluded'. In a perfectly conformist sociality, only anomalous individuals and desocialized categories will be left, and they won't even have any relationship, dialectical or otherwise, with the social institutions. This is what's happening today at an increasingly rapid rate.

As the social sphere is completed, with the discourse on 'the social' playing its part, it expels everyone from the game (the homeless, the unemployed, vagrants, etc., and all the desocialized categories one after the other). In the end, the only people left in the social sphere will be sociologists and social workers, all those for whom the 'social' is their stock in trade, and they will be left grappling with their object, which, though fully realized, has now become virtual. Retrospectively, it will be seen that the social sphere was only ever invented as a place to park the have-nots, and that today they're even being gradually expelled from there, like the Indians being driven off their reservations, thus allowing the better-off classes to occupy the social sphere as a second home. A strange contradictory movement, this, in which there's a growing mismatch between an idealistic, voluntaristic, expert discourse, in which everything's getting better and better by pressing on regardless with imaginary solutions, and the real (if I dare use the term) state of affairs, in which everything's getting inexorably worse. The most disturbing thing is that the two are developing contradictorily and in parallel, with the same irresistible dynamism. Flourishing social provision and galloping exclusion. Educational progress and mental retardation. Perhaps there isn't even a contradiction or distortion here, merely a twist in the same phenomena? This distortion can be seen everywhere: one day the construction of Europe will finally be completed, and there will really be no countries left to be part of it; it will in fact be constructed by successive exclusions and extraditions. It might even be the case, in the end, that when globalism has fully taken shape, and the cycle of information is perfectly integrated, there won't be anyone left on the networks any more. This is the perfect rule – the one where there are only exceptions. The perfect crime: the one in which there are only victims and accomplices, but no murderers (our present condition). The perfect social sphere: the one in which everyone is among 'the excluded'. Perfect communication (the ecstasy of communication): when no one speaks to anyone any more.

PP: Would you accept the idea that, for want of any real physical violence, there is in you an interpretative violence?

JB: Yes, there's a violence of interpretation, and it's positive: it's the very singularity of the analysis. One has to do violence to the facts and the evidence. Systematically to venture the opposite hypothesis to the one accredited by governments and the media, or even by enlightened criticism. For critical thought is extremely fragile in the face of this state of affairs. In any case, it's reality that has to be held in check. The real is what one must not consent to. That reality imposes itself as a principle. Now, the world as it is is not a principle, and has no principle. It simply comes to us, and we come to it. Reality, for its part, has a basis, causes and effects, a rationality – that, indeed, is what makes it a coherent illusion. You can even reproduce it experimentally, if need be. This is what is being undertaken on a grand scale in the name of virtuality, of virtual reality. For the principle of virtuality is a logical extension of the reality principle.

But there can be no question of being parked in that reality, or of taking the real for the real. No question of giving it a status of legitimacy or legality. Or, rather, let's leave it its legal status and go over into illegality. Let's never forget that the real is merely a simulation, a model for regulating and ordering the radical becoming, the radical illusion, of the world and its appearances; for reducing any internal singularity – of events, beings or things – to the common denominator of reality. And if analysis can serve some purpose, it's to resurrect this internal singularity, to put back into play all that has been modelled and remodelled by the reality of the facts. It can serve to recover that *'idiotie transcendantale'* Clément Rosset speaks of, the fateful singularity of the real, instead of this banal idiosyncretism we're locked into.

PP: In *The Perfect Crime*[14] you keep on saying that technology can't have any good final purpose, and you stress that there can be no question of reducing the radical illusoriness of the world. At the same time, you say that there's a ruse of the world just as there's a ruse of history, and that rationality and perfection in general might be said merely to be carrying out its irrational decree. You both denounce the trend towards identification we were speaking of earlier and, at the same time, you wish to save not something of this world, but something of the radical illusion of the world. I'd like to go into this further. I can see that it involves a kind of irony, a sort of roundabout approach, a way of not giving in to the crime of reality, to the disappearance of the world as such as a result of its being identified, highly defined; but, since you employ the expression 'the ruse of the world', how do you live this out, experience it?

JB: I think that ruse, irony, illusion, denial, reversibility, duplicity and radicality aren't simply passions or attributes of the subject or of consciousness. I think all these qualities have passed into things; they are to some extent object passions, and the world plays with us as much as we play with it. It even has the advantage of playing a double game, no doubt, since the objective irony of a world without desire is far superior to our desire and our subjective irony. This is not about alien-ation or some metaphysical fatality, but a game and a duel. The point is not to set a recriminative thinking (which alienation-based thinking always is) against the world's 'criminal' indifference towards us. There are two ways of viewing our con-dition or our destiny. We can either experience the world, including our modern world of technologies and images (for everything I'm saying about the world here relates not to the world as a mental and philosophical abstraction, but to our cur-rent world of events), in terms of alienation, of expropriation, of loss of determination and will, as a negative fatality, including the fatality of history as a failed adventure – that is the conventional critical analysis. Or we can take the view that there is a double game going on: on the one hand, we play at mastering the world through our technologies (and over a much longer period through lan-guage, the intellect and many other things), but on the other hand we might, without knowing it, be partners in another game (though I don't know what the stakes in that game might be). At any rate, we would not be in control of it. There is something like a secret reversion, a showing-through of the illusion of the world in the very techniques we use to transform it – which take on an ironic connotation as a result. The irony of technology: its alleged reality, its palpably high-level performance, much too dazzling to be true, might be said to be the veil of a duplicity that eludes us, a duplicity we might ourselves involuntarily be acting out. Our very language, our essential and most primitive technology, is the place where the definitive ambivalence of the world rebounds on us. So, in all technologies and images, and also in appearances, we don't know whether the object or the world isn't just toying with us. Just as, with thought, we don't know if we're thinking the world or if the world is thinking us. That is the secret of the illusion.

PP: Couldn't it be said that you're a weaver of illusions?

JB: Yes, if illusion is understood, not as simulacrum or unreality, but as something which drives a breach into a world that is too known, too *déjà-vu*, too conventional, too real. The singular, original illusion, the illusion born of the slip, the breakdown, the disruption, the tiniest gap in things. The illusion that colludes with the void, and with the dizzying effect of teetering on the brink. Remaining sensitive to initial conditions, to effects of turbulence, but also keeping a sensitivity to final conditions, a hypersensitivity to final conditions – that is to say, to predestination and the 'fatal', the only way of preserving a passion for the event – for the object and for the event as destiny, not as objective fact.

PP: Doesn't this recovering or teasing-out of appearances and forms go together in you with a desire to disappear? You say: 'There's no point dying, you have to learn how to disappear.' Taking the precise example of information and news, you condemn information because you believe it is total, and leads nowhere except to consensus. Can't one learn to use information?

JB: I don't look for the good or bad use of information. I try to see how that sphere of information condemns itself, contradicts its own principles, destroys itself by a fateful mechanism. It destroys the event, then it destroys itself as event. It's an immense zero-sum circuit.

PP: I come back to news and information. I was watching a documentary on the history of Rwanda yesterday in the 'Mercredis de l'histoire' slot.[15] We know that over the last ten years there have been more and more documentaries on geopolitical matters, and that these have made for a revival of something like a genuine debate on current conflicts. Thanks to these approaches, the force field that a map represents is relatively more accessible to us than it was not so long ago. In seeking to reconfirm the fateful mechanism of information and the news system, don't you leave the reader without any possibility of understanding what's going on in the world a bit better?

JB: What's going on in the world today is, sadly, globalized, and the principle of the globalization of information runs against the universal principle of solidarity. It does so because information exhausts itself within itself, and absorbs its own ends. Television says nothing but: I'm an image, everything's image. The Internet and computers say nothing but: I'm information, everything's information. It's the sign making itself sign, the medium doing its own advertising. The message is immaterial [*indifférent*]: this is the zero degree, the pure form of communication. All this assumes current political significance, for it's on the basis of message, content, meaning and value that the universal is built. Globalization is built on the basis of the supremacy of the medium and the neutralization of the message. '*La pensée unique*'[16] is 'media'-thinking: the market, the Internet, the information superhighways – uninterrupted circulation. Global integration is achieved on the basis of nullity, of the lowest definition of the message (of meaning, of ideas, of ideology). It's the medium which says least, signifies least; it's the medium which is coextensive with insignificance, with the banality of the operational world. Thus, the media and information broke the 'neither true nor false' barrier long ago, since everything in them depends on instant credibility, with passage into the media itself cancelling the index of reference and truth. This lack of discrimination between the true and the false moves out from there to invade all registers: the aesthetic register of the artwork, the historical register of objectivity, of memory, the political register of opinion, and even the scientific register of proof (the undecidability of an experiment like Jacques Benveniste's on the memory of water[17]).

If there's no longer either true or false, lying becomes impossible and, with it, all the artifices of perversion and seduction. We are – like it or not – in the position of agnostics, where it's not a question of believing or not believing, since everything is in the making-believe, and is wholly consumed in this credibility effect. Opinion polls and advertising are neither true nor false, just as fashion is neither beautiful nor ugly. Truth-effects, beauty-effects, etc., have slipped their moorings and become statistical, random.

In fractal space (but equally today in historical space), things are no longer one-, two- or three-dimensional; they float in an interstitial dimension. You launch a news item. So long as it has not been denied, it is plausible. Barring accidents, it will never be denied in real time. Even if it is denied later, it will never again be absolutely false, since it has once enjoyed credibility. Unlike truth, credibility cannot be refuted, since it is virtual. We are in a kind of fractal truth: just as a fractal object no longer has one or two dimensions, but $1 \cdot 2$ or $2 \cdot 3$ dimensions, so an event is no longer true or false, but oscillates between $1 \cdot 2$ and $2 \cdot 3$ octaves of truth. The space between the true and the false is no longer a relational space, but a space of random distribution.

PP: Where is this fractal truth leading us?

JB: This shift of dimensions leads to a shift in responsibility. Responsibility is not dead: it has become viral. Truth is not dead: it has become viral and elusive – disease itself has become viral. Even sexuality, which floats today in a strange interstitial dimension that is neither masculine nor feminine, but somewhere between the two: $1 \cdot 2 - 1 \cdot 7$. There's no sexual definition any longer; hence no longer, strictly speaking, any sexual difference. The uncertainty principle is at the very heart of sexual life, as it is at the heart of all value systems.

Free now of their polar opposites, everyone can ratchet up their own powers and multiply their effects. The true becomes truer than true. The false becomes falser than false. Even the neither-true-nor-false – the zero degree, insignificance – can be raised to the higher power in a kind of Dutch auction of nullity, a sort of raising of banality to the power x, as can be verified every day in art, political discourse, the exacerbation of kitsch and nonsense, the logical non-differentiation between opposing value-terms being reflected in our own indifference, our emotional, psychological, political indifference – an indifference intensified by being caught up in its own game, culminating in a kind of fever of indifference – an indifference that has become a kind of collective virus, a kind of fanatical behaviour which can lead to violent effects such as are usually the effects of passion, so true is it that insignificance can become aggravated, that the nothing can get carried away with itself and that things can intensity in the void; this might even be said to be what drives our banality.

Information, for example, is truer than true, it's true in real time; that's why it is fundamentally uncertain. In that uncertainty, which is the product of an excess of positivity, the only vital reaction is rejection. As a result of the excess of information, the excess of moralizing, the excess of rationalization of the world, only evil is certain; good is never certain. Only the false is certain; the true is never certain. In the ambiguity of values, it's always the false that wins out. It's our only recourse against undecidability, against the disappearance of truth-criteria. When, for example, criteria of aesthetic distinction disappear (as in the appreciation of current art), everything shifts on to the question of authenticity or falsehood. Authenticity, the signature of a work, wins out over its value; everything becomes centred on the expert appraisal and, naturally, this superstitious pursuit of authenticity becomes the basis of market value, the basis of an unlimited speculation. The laws of the market totter at the same time as the criteria of aesthetic value. When we speak of authenticity, the false has virtually won out. When we speak of morality (of the 'truth' of products, etc.), immorality has virtually won out. When we speak of human rights, etc. . . . .

PP: Destabilization doesn't necessarily mean renunciation. The denunciation of the belief in the possibility of a 'final solution' of all human problems has – as P.-A. Taguieff suggests in *Les Fins de l'anti-racisme* – also been a constant of our political culture since Herzen.

JB: This infiltration, this contamination of all values, is universal. Even in the historical field, objectivity can be contaminated by a kind of virus which today makes it possible to express doubt over the reality of the gas chambers. Even when it is violently denied, this doubt impacts upon minds, which is something previously unthinkable. Computer viruses prefigure a virtual destabilization of all information, just as other viruses prefigure a destabilization of sexual life. The destabilization of political life: in the absence of criteria of choice and opinion, imaginations (or, rather, the probability screens which stand in for political imagination) are captivated by opinion poll figures. Economic destabilization: the unreal economy of speculation overlays and debases real economies by substituting for them an exacerbated simulation – the simulation of capital flows. Here again, this virtual economy is neither true nor false; there is nothing to set against it. It is by denial of its own rules, its own purposes, that it becomes invulnerable, dissuasive of the real economy, and perfectly autonomous. But it isn't invulnerable to the viruses it engenders as a consequence of its very autarky, its 'trans-economic' immunity: it is becoming autoimmune and, consequently, prey to a different pathology.

One makes every effort to protect oneself from this triumph of undecidability, which ushers in the transparence of falsehood, just as the permeability of good and evil ushers in the transparence of evil by resuscitating by all available means the paradigm of the authenticity of the fact, the evidence, the origin, the reference. If what is at stake in thought disappears, it becomes crucial to fall back upon objectivity, upon a paternity suit. Hence the compulsive pursuit of veracity, verification, documentation, clarification and objective rehabilitation which grips every field, quite clearly as a result of thought's weakness in confronting that undecidability in any other way than through a history. Sadly, even history plays us false, even history today is party to the uncertainty. Uncertainty brings with it a mad race, a pursuit-race, between means of detection and means of falsification, between viruses and protective measures (in art, in credit cards, in computing, in the protection of ideas, but also in sex, where we are all now liable to AIDS testing – an expansion of the general test of authenticity). This is our new original sin, which is exactly the opposite of the other, the knowledge of good and evil. That was, ultimately, a blessing from heaven which made us human. The curse which is upon us lies in the impossibility of distinguishing between good and evil, true and false. Adam and Eve had fallen into the moral anxiety of distinction; we have fallen into the immoral panic of indistinction, of the confusion of all criteria. Of the contamination of good by evil, and vice versa. And the virus is the symptom of this. Our entry into the age of the virus through our inability to distinguish between values is equivalent to the expulsion of our ancestors from the earthly paradise for the opposite reason of knowledge of good and evil.

And, given that loss of immunity, all the lethal infections are lying in wait for us, all the sins from the primal scene are resurfacing, all the viruses dormant in our cells are reawakened as the crisis takes hold! Our impotence in the face of the dispersion of values, their fractal dissemination, is much worse than the ancient moral responsibility which weighed on our consciences.

PART TWO

In Search of Lost Forms

Chapter 5
America, America . . .

Philippe Petit: Rereading *America* (1986), I was struck by the similarity between your approach and Sartre's text on New York in *Situations*. Your vision of America is based on the same perceptions as his. In his text, Sartre contrasted the low, heavy skies of Paris with the untamed sky of New York, the narrow streets and the great avenues, the European city and the American city, in the way you contrast the policed society of the Europeans and the primitive society of the Americans. Did your desire to write *America* arise out of weariness with old Europe? Did you feel the need, like Sartre, to break with it and immerse yourself in the American desert in order to be reborn a little? Do you still have the same admiration for the land of Roosevelt?

Jean Baudrillard: I wrote it at the point when I was beginning, not to detach myself from America, but to have travelled right around it. The writing took over from the travel. It wasn't linked to the desire to compare the United States and Europe. I wasn't tempted by a historical or cultural comparison. What I was observing was another scene, a primal scene. In *America*, I wasn't trying to get at an American entity or essence, but at another world. For me, it was a kind of otherness or fascination. It wasn't the political or economic reality which interested me, but that sort of transfiguration of banality characteristic of a new continent – not just new geographically, but mentally. I experienced it on a cinema screen, as it were, hypothesizing almost experimentally a country without a history.

PP: When you began writing *America*, you were teaching at Santa Barbara?

JB: Santa Barbara was towards the end. It all began in 1970 with an international design congress. Then came New York and California. I taught at San Diego, then at Los Angeles for three months. That was the eye-opening moment. This was in 1975. I was offered a post, but I never wanted to settle there. It was too much responsibility and I wanted, in a sense, to remain irresponsible. Once you get stuck in the deep America of the campuses. . . . When I was at San Diego, Lyotard, Marin and de Certeau were there. It was a great time.

PP: Were you struck at San Diego by the difference between the American students and students at Nanterre?

JB: Greatly. I went there with the idea that California was a testing ground of simulation, but the experimental side wasn't so much there as in the deserts. As for social and university life, unlike Nanterre, where we'd just been through an extraordinary period, a violent phase of cultural, ideological and political liberation, there was an easy-going fluid lifestyle over there, as though liberation were already far in the past. You had the impression of having physically passed beyond that permanent revolution, which was always ideological and utopian, and never achieved. Over there, it was made reality – made hyperreality, of course: that was the paradox. American students were extraordinarily willing, but they didn't understand much about the discourse of the simulacrum. In a way they embodied it, but they didn't analyse it. I made a kind of ethereal commentary on it, a bit extraterrestrial. I was the one who seemed like an extraterrestrial. But everything went very well, in spite of this disparity. In any case, as soon as I had a free moment, I went off into the desert. For me, that was the real scene.

PP: Your book opens with the desert, alongside the theme of the extermination of meaning to which you return throughout the work. Did the desert initiate this quest for the death of meaning?

JB: Yes, it's a kind of infinite perspective, an extreme form of renunciation of the world [*dépouillement*], which is more than the state of nature. It isn't culture, either. It's even the most radical form of counter-culture. It's a way of sweeping away all the cultural superstructures: a sort of hyperspace, of degree zero of the object and meaning, a sort of mental geology. It wasn't the Indians I was after. It was the desert cadenced by speed, the plane, the car, the heat, the surface radiance, physical and metaphysical.

PP: That experimental field initiated you into mysticism. I'm thinking of Meister Eckhart's mysticism and the expression 'radical indifference' which struck me. You write: 'Desert: luminous, fossilized network of an inhuman intelligence, of a radical indifference − the indifference not merely of the sky, but of the geological undulations, where the metaphysical passions of space and time crystallize.'[1] If we pressed this radical indifference, it's a theme we'd find again in the Rhenish mystics and a number of modern thinkers. One has the impression that it runs through all your thinking. I wouldn't say there's a will to indifference, but at any rate a pursuit of this radical indifference.

JB: It was a reaction to what I would call the snobbery of difference, the snobbery of European culture, which is built upon every kind of distinction, including distinctions between moral values. Through objects and simulacra, I had moved towards an indifference between good and evil. Not a subjective indifference, but an objective indifference of the world, and a radical insignificance of the subject in that world of pure signs that is the desert. Actually, we aren't far here from certain mystical forms of renunciation of the world, but in this case it wasn't a matter of transcendence, but only of the world, of the absolute self-evidence of the world. The desert is a trap, the trap of space, the trap of appearances. All the values and categories of the mind get caught in this trap and cancel themselves automatically. In the civilized world, if you want to begin to think with a certain freedom you have to make a considerable effort. You find yourself immediately with your back to the wall of difference and culture. Whereas there, I could vanish into the indifference of the world.

PP: That indifference goes together with a sort of suspension of transcendence. There is perhaps another word which would help us to understand your approach: the word 'immanence'. You are more on the side of immanence than transcendence.

JB: Yes, on the side of – not a phenomenological, but almost a phenomenal, reduction of things. You never, in fact, escape transcendence, any more than you escape discourse, but at a given point the lighting changes, and even ideas pass by in the landscape like unidentified objects. Everything is restored to its raw self-evidence, its quality as pure event – a kind of immanence, but one which might be said to have retained the quality and energy of transcendence.

PP: Deleuze used the expression 'transcendence in immanence'.

JB: Transcendence is always required to deny or surpass itself, and how would it surpass itself except into immanence? There was, indeed, something sacrificial in that – the joyous sacrifice of transcendence. But the Americans didn't by any means accept this reversal of their image, in which they became extras in a kind of inhuman fiction. They couldn't bear to be seen as a primitive society. For me, it was praise, a mark of great inspiration. I believed I was allying with something other than deep America, allying with a 'primitive' self-evidence of the modern world. With us, everything is always philosophical – even the glorification of appearances against depth . . . all the Nietzschean themes are experienced philosophically. Over there, even theory becomes once again what it is: a fiction.

PP: Did you read American literature over there?

JB: I read more American fiction than French, not to mention the films. But the key point is that any difference between fiction and daily life fades away. Over there, even literature and cinema, screen fiction, are part of the continent. It's a country I've never felt nostalgic for, but in all the time I was travelling around it I never felt homesick for Europe.

PP: This ease of living comes back to what you were saying. An innocence of the body, a freedom acquired, not won. When you experienced this bodily ease, how did you see it? As an extension of childhood?

JB: It's a kind of trancelike state. Akin to an indifference that is not a repudiation or renunciation of meaning, but a 'beyond' of difference, made up of the multiplicity of languages and landscapes, the availability of space. A singular, spacious freedom, the liberty no longer to be grappling with your own image. A freedom much more spatial than philosophical, a mobile liberty, the liberty of the body and movement. A transitive liberty, linked to the accelerated reciprocity of things in speed. It's true also of cities and individuals. Once you've escaped from the constraints of the universities, whether you're in New York or Los Angeles, you have a total spectacle of the life of individuals. You can decipher their whole existence in the transparency of their banality. With us, that transparency is melancholy and depressive. Over there, it ends up being an event. All the qualities and conditions which are negative for us are reborn over there in a kind of innocence and scope which gives them the potency of a natural phenomenon. Banality, too, is a desert, and you can travel through it in the same way as you would travel the outer reaches of our phenomenal world. With us, freedom is something won from the social sphere, through conflict and compromise. Over there, you have the impression that there's too much for everyone – it's even a problem – but at least, when utopia is achieved, you can use it with a lightness of touch.

PP: Isn't that the innocence of power? A casualness which can emerge only because it's borne along by power?

JB: Naturally, you can express this in terms of global privilege. It's true that

America affords itself the luxury of being a kind of primitive society, of enjoying an immoral power and innocence. And you can afford yourself the luxury of enjoying America in the same way, the luxury of forgetting the relation of forces and living out prosperity like an unreal situation. The same violence and contradictions exist over there, but it's their overexposure that makes the difference. The difference between the real and the more-real-than-real, between the banal and the more-banal-than-banal, between the violent and the more-violent-than-violent – and this even includes the obese, who are fatter than fat. Even business is a show there, even capitalism has turned into spectacle; it surpasses itself in crazed speculation, whereas we merely afford ourselves the shamefaced comedy of modernity and the political.

PP: You stressed American banality. Part of your book is devoted to Tocqueville. You push him towards his logical end, writing of 'a world that has shown genius in its irrepressible development of equality, banality, and indifference'.[2] Equality here is Tocqueville; banality and indifference is you?

JB: Though in Tocqueville there's already an analysis of this democratic erosion. It's because people are individualized and equal before the law that they become indifferent to each other.

PP: Your view of Tocqueville leads to the idea that America is the country which achieves the end of political ideology. Is this historical naivety of the Americans a naivety against Europe?

JB: I'd say that, instead of taking the road to Abyssinia, I took the road to California. You have to leave Europe. It just happened to be that country. There's no predestination, other than the retrospective. I could have landed up somewhere else. There is always, of course, the imaginary power of America as the 'cutting edge'. But the essential thing was to escape from Europe metaphysically, far from a nostalgic culture and history. To escape to reaches where our history is both cancelled out and multiplied to excess. To pursue the European destiny in its extremities, its excrescences, its monstrosities. To find an end-of-race, end-of-history electricity. To infiltrate into a non-culture which was both the parody of European cultures and one which checkmated them – by 'discovered' check, as it were.

They have originality. We don't have it any more. Europe's outgrowth into colonialism has exhausted it. It will never recover. One can easily see how wrong it is even to reconstitute the idea. Europe has expropriated itself in its colonial worlds, which have become autonomous and, in relation to it and its outdated culture, worlds of power, science fiction worlds. I'd have liked to have been a Jesuit in California in the seventeenth century or in Paraguay in the sixteenth, close to the original event, the cultural and anthropological event, which (short of waiting for the backlash of the rest of the world against the Western world) will never come again. Perhaps the heroic anthropologists still found a glimmer of this in the nineteenth century. This is what America was for me. Latin America could be that, too, but for that another imagination than mine is needed.

PP: You're referring to Las Casas's encounter with the Indians?

JB: There won't really be an anthropological surprise like that again. The only equivalent would be in our running into a species other than the human in the same way. Moreover, the shock wave from that event isn't fully played out, and we're perhaps very subtly seeing, in the long term, a revenge of what Borges called the 'mirror peoples'.[3]

PP: One gets the impression that, in your view, there's no longer a living European culture.

JB: It's true that there's a bias here towards a break with the culture at hand and a steadily growing allergy to the French and European world (particularly in its current tendencies). But I made that choice very early on, even intellectually. In the field of ideas, I carried out a kind of symbolic murder, made an umbilical break. At the origin, there's always this brutal, irrational drive to repudiate what is near (including the real world), so as to go and look elsewhere – and to precipitate things towards their ends, so as to go and look beyond.

PP: Was America a springboard for what you call the transpolitical?

JB: It's true that over there, there's not even the notion of a political revolution like ours. From the outset you're in the transpolitical sphere of the medium and the screen, which – fortunately or otherwise – exempts you from any social realism. You can think whatever you like about this hegemony of the medium, but at least it's a total social fact. Whereas in our traditional world, we retain the sentimental cult of the message. The – ideological, political, psychological or cultural – message streams out everywhere. In our confessional TV shows everyone plays out their televisual tragicomedy. Only the existential malaise comes over on the medium. In fact, television has been sacrificed as a medium, sacrificed to a kind of realism, a kind of realist banality of the message. More exactly, if the medium destroys the message and meaning, the message in its turn destroys the power of the medium – which makes information a zero-sum signification. All this drowned in the indistinct form of culture. In America, I had the impression of encountering the medium, the media in their potency and primitiveness.

PP: Has America, your America, changed since those years?

JB: America has changed, but it remains a field in which a *de facto*, untamed multiculturality is in play, and this seems more interesting to me than finding the way of dividing things up that would reconcile everyone. That being said, when I knew it, it was still a specific, original object. America is everywhere now – by media injection, so to speak – in all latitudes and countries. You run into America now only in the form of a global drip-feed.

PP: And Eastern Europe, the Caucasus, Russia? You've never been tempted to get into those places?

JB: I can't see how I would make the adjustment to another world. Latin America is fascinating. It gives every impression of never having to find a political, economic or social reality principle, which today, when all these principles are in total confusion, is an absolute advantage. So, some large countries, which are termed underdeveloped, are perhaps in the van, in that they've skipped all these phases of modernity in which we're trapped today. Perhaps it's better not to have passed through the political, economic or social mirror-stage, which is also the stage of the entrapping mirror of democratic evolutionism. At any rate, the hybridization of languages, races and religions gives the impression of a world in fusion, not one on a drip-feed [*en perfusion*] like our own. As for the countries of Eastern Europe, they're doubtless experiencing 'descending' history, the repeting of history, more virulently than we are. We have before us in Russia the whole of the twentieth century, as it has made and unmade itself right or wrong side out, and the memory blowback is much more violent than it is here, much more archaic. It is, therefore, a more radical situation than ours, in spite of the disarray and confusion that prevail.

PP: Yet you choose to live in France?

JB: It's an automatic choice, out of inertia. So what – I'm European. I'm condemned to a kind of objective, historical nihilism. You're forced to admit to yourself that everything radical you can do or say in this society will only ever be the radicality of this corrupt society. You'll never have any other truth to tell than that which concerns this society at a given moment. There's no freedom to be conquered from the inside any longer; there's nothing more to be conquered from the inside. Better to move into another world, into a radical otherness which doesn't need you to exist, an otherness for which America is the metaphor.

PP: 'As against the melancholy of European analyses'. . . . Is America still, for you, the land of achieved utopia?

JB: America does still have within it something of the excess and magical paradox of achieved utopia. Without illusions: that utopia is the utopia of achieved banality, and hence of a transversal equivalence of everything and a levelled-down equality of destiny. But this – which is in any case the inevitable fate of modernity, and of which we have only the depressive aspect – has been elevated by the Americans into an event, which is perhaps, in actual fact, the event of the end of history, or in other words, contrary to the way Fukuyama has it, its definitive non-accomplishment.

PP: A last question on America, since you've just come back from there. Do you still agree with the passage in your book in which you wrote: 'For me there is no truth of America. I ask of the Americans only that they be Americans. I do not ask them to be intelligent, sensible, original. I ask them only to populate a space incommensurate with my own, to be for me the highest sidereal point, the finest orbital space'?[4]

JB: Yes.

Chapter 6
'Photos are very beautiful, but you mustn't say so . . .'

Philippe Petit: Reading your writings on photography, one has the feeling you are replaying the passionate nineteenth-century quarrel on the art of photography. I'm thinking of a comment by Ingres: 'Photos are very beautiful, but you mustn't say so . . .', and of Walter Benjamin saying that you couldn't reflect on photography 'without first wondering whether the very invention of photography had not over-turned the fundamental character of art completely'. You seem to adopt that approach as your own. It isn't so much photography you reject, but photography's becoming image, like art becoming gallery art, as we have already discussed. That's what put me in mind of Ingres's comment.

Jean Baudrillard: It's true that there is in photography a secret to be preserved. I speak of this as an untutored, intermittent user and practitioner. What I regret is the aestheticization of photography, and that this type of image has become one of the fine arts, and fallen into the abyss of culture. The photographic image came, by its technical essence, from a region before or beyond aesthetics, and by that token it constitutes a considerable revolution in our mode of representation. The irrup-tion of photography throws art itself into question in its aesthetic monopoly of the image. Now, it is art which has swallowed up photography rather than the other way round (it has paid the price for this, since it has gradually emptied itself of its substance). Photography comes from elsewhere, and must remain there. It is part of another, timeless tradition which is not, properly speaking, aesthetic, and which is the tradition of *trompe-l'œil* that runs right through the history of art, but does so indifferent to its twists and turns. *Trompe-l'œil* is linked to the self-evidence of the world, and to such a minutely detailed resemblance that it's only apparently realistic (it is, in fact, magical). It preserves the magical status of the image, whereas art lapses into aesthetics, following a progression which leads from the sacred to the beautiful, then to generalized aesthetics. Now, the anthropological power of the image stands opposed to well-tempered representation and to any realist vision – it retains something of the radical illusion of the world.

It is, therefore, an instinctive [*sauvage*] form, irreducible to the aestheticization of things, linked to their appearance, their self-evidence – but to a deceptive self-evidence. It runs quite contrary to the twofold goal that's been foisted upon it: realism or aestheticism. For me, a photographic image is still valid today not so much in terms of quality or content as in terms of pure fascination. It's closer to the origin and the torments of representation. By dint of the non-realist play with technique, and by its definitive excision, its absolute stillness, its silence, its phenomenological reduction of colour and movement, it is the purest and most artificial image. It isn't beautiful, it's worse. And it's as such that it assumes the force of an object in a world in which precisely the aesthetic principle is petering out. And so I've got caught up in the game of this fetishistic immanence of the object, and this convergence between an objective technique and the very potency of the object. The photographic operation is a sort of reflex, a sort of automatic writing of the self-evidence of the world – a self-evidence which is really nothing of the kind.

PP: For you, photography is a primitive art, a savage art. You say: 'All the other forms of image, far from being advances, are perhaps only attenuated forms of this break between the pure image and the real.' It's no accident either if, later in this same text on primitiveness and the stupefaction which arises out of the photographic art, the only literary references you make are to Gombrowicz and Nabokov.

JB: It's because they represent something which goes beyond the dimension of literature, aesthetics and any well-tempered culture. I would say the same of Bacon in the field of art. The powerful works are those which no longer play-act art, aesthetics and culture. In the field of thought, they are those which no longer play-act ideas, interpretation and meaning.

To get back to photography: it's technics which gives the photo its extraordinary character as image. It's through this technicity that our world reveals itself to be radically non-objective. It is, paradoxically, the objective lens of the camera which reveals the unobjectivity of the world, that little something which will not be resolved by analysis or in resemblance. By its technique, it carries us beyond resemblance, to the heart of the illusion of reality. In so doing, it also transforms the vision we have of technics. We're taken here beyond the moral or philosophical rejection of 'alienating' technics to a perspective on it as the strategic site of a double game, as the magnifying mirror of illusion and forms. From that perspective, the question becomes: do we think the world or does the world think us? Through photography, it's the object which is looking at us, thinking us. At least, that's how it would be if photography hadn't been reduced to the level of an aesthetic practice.

PP: That puts me in mind of the relationship between man and machine as conceived by Simondon, who made a distinction between technics and technology. Denigrators of technics today often confuse technics with technology. What Simondon called technical culture and technical individuals is the possibility we find in Marey and others of a strong exchange between man and machine. The machine is first a challenge to man, before it's an obstacle or a panacea.

JB: There's a duel between technical equipment and the world, and a collusion too (the one implies the other). Photography (but not just photography, of course) might be said to be the art of slipping into that collusion – not to control the process, but to play with it and show that the die is not irrevocably cast. Is this true of technics as a whole? At any rate, it's the way to turn around the conventional view of it.

PP: Photography is the objectal; it's the object looking at us rather than the subject looking. How do you move from this technical view of photography to this para-aesthetic view?

JB: I don't appeal to an inverted, object-based aesthetics. I'm not saying the object has taken control. Turning things round here means making the object, on which the subject's presence and representation are imposed, the site of the absence and disappearance of the subject; so, it means making the object emerge as an indissoluble self-evidence. The photographic 'object' may, in fact, be a situation, a quality of light or a living creature. The key thing is that it should take on the force of a pure event or object and, to do that, the subject has to have withdrawn from it. Somewhere in this over-perfectly designed machinery of representation, there has to be a fracture. The object's priority shatters the scenario of representation (and, of course, all the moral and philosophical dialectics attaching to it). It's an inversion of the mirror. Until now it was the subject which was the mirror of representation; the object was merely the content. This time, it's the object which says 'I shall be your mirror' – that is to say: 'I (We) shall be your favourite disappearing act'. The subject forfeits the monopoly of interpretation. Or, rather, no interpretation is possible any longer. As the object has nothing to say and is without desire, its power, which is that of the uncoffering of the world in the raw state, cannot be distilled or negotiated in commentary or interpretation. For the object to be grasped, the subject has to loose his grasp on himself. But this provides the subject with his last adventure, his last chance, the chance to be dispossessed of himself not in traditional alienation, but in the reverberation of a world in which he occupies what is, from now on, the blind place of representation. The object, for its part, has a much greater power of play since, not having passed through the mirror-stage, it doesn't have to deal with its image, its identity or its resemblance. The object scoffs at all these problems in which the subject is bogged down today, as it scoffs at desire (this is also true of the sexual 'object'). If one manages to capture something of this objective dissimilarity and singularity, something of the world changes – not only within the real, but beyond its reality principle.

PP: What you say of the object also goes for the photographed subject. In a passage on the heroic age of photography, you say of the subject that he has the stature of the dead. Well, nowadays, in your view, the nothingness has disappeared from images, from photography. Is this why there's no photographic art any more?

JB: This business about the dead is quite simply the idea that at the heart of the photographic image there's a figure of nothingness, of absence, of unreality. It's this nothingness at the heart of the image which gives it its magic. It's this nothingness which has been expelled in all possible ways, by saturating the photo with all manner of references and significations. Photo-reportage festivals and galleries are chock-full of eyewitness accounts, aesthetic or demagogic sentimentality, stereotypes. It's a positive prostitution of the image to what it signifies, the image taken hostage by its own content. In the profusion of our images, death and violence are everywhere, but a pathos-laden, ideological, spectacular death. By contrast, what Barthes calls the '*punctum*', that absent point, that nothingness at the heart of the image which gives it its power, no longer exists. And this seems to me an error, even from the point of view of the message, for no wretchedness or violence in the world impinges on us if we have removed this specificity of the image, this symbolic void which gives it its potency. This is also why it is so difficult to photograph human beings, living beings, because they are themselves so charged with meaning that it's almost impossible to set it aside to find the secret form of their absence.

PP: Can you clarify what you mean by secret otherness here, because many authors have spoken of the secret, from the most psychological – Gide, say – to the least psychological, such as Deleuze? It's sometimes difficult to know what they all mean by this. What do you mean by secret otherness? Is this why you don't like photographers who, when they're doing your portrait, try to put you at ease with small talk?

JB: Yes, because, in a total psychological misconception, they think they're bringing out your deep identity. Only bad actors identify with their roles. They try to use unsubtle tricks to bring out a truth of the person or the face. Now, to grasp someone in their singularity is to grasp in them what is beyond their own grasp, to grasp the way they escape your grasp. Each person is doubtless present with their will and desire, but, secretly, their decisions and thoughts come to them from elsewhere, and it's in this very strange interaction that their originality lies. It isn't in the mirrors in which they recognize themselves, nor in the lens that's trying to recognize them. The trap is always the trap of resemblance, and what's interesting in the image, when it knows how to preserve its secrecy (and this also goes for cinema and painting), is that it defies all resemblance, that it seeks elsewhere what comes from elsewhere. Something's in play which one has to grasp before it takes on the appearance of determination and meaning. In our lives we rely to a considerable extent on the machinery of will and representation, but the real story goes on elsewhere.

PP: Does this non-resemblance connect with what Blanchot called 'cadaverous resemblance'?[5]

JB: I don't know. I would speak, rather, of a kind of metapsychology, a metapsychology in which we are never a single individual, in which we are born in the dual state and each of us is haunted by his own twin, the true resolution of the Oedipus complex no longer being the separation from the mother and father, but the separation from the original twin. That double has to be exorcized, conjured away, if one is to be oneself, and perhaps we never truly succeed in this. We're haunted by this phantom twinness, by this identical reduplication, and we're always under threat of merging into it. This is why otherness from elsewhere, any kind of seduction from elsewhere, frees us from the fateful presence of this phantom twin (this alternative is shown very powerfully in the film *Dead Ringers*). Those who remain attached to it are dead in life – and this we all are after a fashion, caught in the trap of a maleficent identity. Singularity can come only from splitting and a breaking of symmetry.

PP: Can one name this phantom twin? Why a double, and not triplets? Why do you stress this theme of the double?

JB: We conceive the world of individuation being surpassed only in plurality or multiplicity. That way, we remain in the same accounting register. The one and the more-than-one, the one and the many, the singular and the plural. Now, there's a fundamental form which is neither unity nor plurality: an original, irreducible form which is duality. It can disappear into multiplicity or dissemination or, conversely, into individuality, that species of artificial totality. But the living, antagonistic form remains the dual form – a specific mode in some languages, but one that has almost disappeared from ours. A primordial relation this, which is not the one multiplied by two, nor the dialectical or interactive mode of the one to the other – a dual form, irreducible to the one and the other, which is there from the outset in a symbolic reciprocity. Life is, of course, a double game for escaping the dual within the individual, but it's geared, all the same, to the irruption of this secret otherness.

PP: If I follow you, your ideal would be for a photographer to capture your phantom twin?

JB: For my part, I've never found either the twin form or the dual form in the photos of myself that I've seen. Who knows? I must have a resistance of the same order as my resistance to psychoanalysis. I'm as difficult to photograph as I am to analyse. Having said this, the human for us is ultimately conflated with the individual. With the duality I'm speaking of we enter, in a sense, upon the inhuman, with all that this implies in terms of fascination and danger. However, some manage to sense this otherness in other people through photography. Sometimes a single detail, an angle, a quality of light, can bring this about. For if, taken all in all, the individual is quite conventional, taken in the detail, in the fragment – it's the same with the world – he or she is always original.

PP: If you can't name this phantom twin, can you render it poetically?

JB: That otherness doesn't necessarily come from others; it can arise out of a situation, an event, from all kinds of strange seductions and convergences, from anything which breaks this twin symmetry. In the past, other powers, for good or ill, saw to it that we were dissociated from ourselves, whereas now everyone is left to him/herself. Everyone is caught in the trap of him/herself, even in the minutiae of life, in the debris of that now-lost symbolic organization. Everyone is merely the mirror of the other in the broken mirror of alterity.

Through technics, the human world has entered upon the inhuman. When everyone becomes a technical vehicle, an operational vector of the same networks, what was still merely the tragic destiny of twins becomes the curse of clones.

PP: There remains, none the less, an extraordinary specificity of human thought, which perhaps comes down to the fact that it has taken up residence in science as much as in duration, to paraphrase Bergson: science is the distinctive feature of man; it is of the essence of the human. Man is the only being who can build a theory of himself. François Laruelle describes man as a theoretical individual.

JB: The human has been defined for only two or three centuries, and it was defined very intellectually, in terms of reason. Since then, the relation to the world has been through that extremely subtle organ, the brain. In other cultures the relation to the world is a relation of the whole body, caught in the cycle of metamorphoses, and in collusion with the world. Our modern, rational intelligence makes us technical beings from the very start, beings in the image of our tools and knowledge. Now, it seems that today our technologies and sciences go way beyond human intellection. Who knows if they're not carrying us towards a new relationship, a new set of rules based on radical uncertainty? This implies a kind of sacrifice of the intellect, a sort of brutal interruption in the cycle of the species. There are some fine pages in Saul Bellow on the fact that our civilization now lives in self-hatred – a self-hatred arising out of insuperable remorse at this break with the species. It's the continuity of the species in us that is being avenged for the fact that we've become free, emancipated individuals. We're still continuing to expiate that betrayal. Our modernity is defined by the perspective of humanism and the Enlightenment, but what preceded us is far more immense than that humanism, and knew nothing of this distinction between the human and the inhuman. The discovery – or rediscovery – of the inhuman, the violence done to the human in the current field of knowledge, seems to me to be more than an opening, a breach through which to explore the inhuman potentialities of man, and to rediscover – who knows? – a possible metamorphosis of the species, other than its artificial survival in technology.

PP: Do you agree with Susan Sontag's assertion that 'Cameras are the antidote and the disease, a means of appropriating reality and a means of making it obsolete'?[6]

JB: Why not? But all these formulas are reductive, in so far as they always revolve around the real – the problem being to exorcize or appropriate it. Once again, in the generic illusion of the image, for better or for worse the problem of the real no longer arises. It's left behind in the very movement of the image which, from the outset, passes beyond the true and the false, the real and the unreal. The image isn't a medium for which we have to find the right use. It is what it is and, as such, it escapes all our moral considerations. It's immoral in its essence, and the world's becoming image is an immoral development. It's up to us to escape our representation, and become ourselves the immoral vectors of the image. It's up to us to become objects again, to become other again in a relation of seduction with the world.

PP: I'd like to come back to the word 'primitive'. You say: 'For objects, savages, beasts, primitives, alterity is certain, singularity is certain; the most insignificant of objects is other, for subjects it is much less certain.'

JB: Savages are not necessarily primitives. What is savage is what is not confronted with its resemblance, with its identity, with the desperate search for that identity. A beast doesn't have an identity. It's all the others together, and it's not itself. For all that, it's not alienated: it's foreign to itself, foreign to its own meaning, foreign to its own end. Consequently, it has this charm of beings which are foreign to their image, but enjoy an organic familiarity with their bodies and an organic complicity with all the others. If one manages to recover this connivance and this strangeness, one approaches a poetic quality of otherness, a poetry of alterity similar to that of paradoxical sleep (identity being the equivalent of deep sleep).

PP: In speaking of the magic of photography, you stress its phenomenal stillness. Isn't this possibility of unparalleled contemplation which photography offers us a quasi-Zen way, in your writing, of breaking with Western transcendence and seeking a more Eastern attitude?

JB: I certainly wouldn't say 'Eastern', because I don't want to play on words or references. There's a kind of effect of stupefaction, if not of contemplation, in the image and the photograph. The 'freeze-frame' is in this sense a freezing of the world. The image interrupts the rush of events. This kind of 'suspense' is never definitive, since photos are never there singly, and refer on from one to another (the image has no other destiny than the image), with this kind of stillness and silence in common. This is doubtless why photography has reacquired an extraordinary aura, which it had lost when cinema came along. But cinema also – in the work of Godard, for example – can recover this specific quality of the image: collusive with, but foreign to, narration; static, but harnessing all the energy of movement. In this sense, photographs offer an example of a high degree of condensation, the condensation of a whole course of events in a fixed image, whereas most current images offer the example of great dilution.

PP: Ideally, you say, photography should do without commentary, and you don't show much fondness for the institutions which celebrate it. Do you think that kind of institution is a nuisance? Do you think it contributes to diluting the force of the image rather than restoring that force to its full dimensions?

JB: The image is offstage, 'out-of-shot', the opposite of staging. The staging of photographs, whether aesthetic or institutional, their staging in exhibitions and museums, is a nonsense. With official embalming by the museum, and the solemnity of the cult of photography, you get the bizarre impression that that death we were speaking of, the death at the heart of the image, has left it, been expelled from it, and has taken on the outward form of a mausoleum or necropolis. Instead of the image symbolically enclosing death, death closes around the image.

PP: On Bacon, who photographed himself in his photo-booth shots, you say the best subjects to photograph themselves are those who have found their obsessive form, their temperamental identity, their narcissistic aspect [*figure*]. Would you say of the painter Bacon that he succeeded in photographing himself in his photo-booth pictures?

JB: I don't know what place that had in his work. I think one can – and Bacon is the example of this – no longer regard oneself at all as a representative being, but as an obsessive, temperamental being/object, working in one's own cycle, and not in any sense in a staging of oneself. Bacon went quite a long way in that frenzied self-delimitation. There's a touch of enchantment in this, which you can also find in acting, in which you go beyond your own image and you are left to a kind of happy fatality. It's you – and it isn't you – who are acting at that moment. Some people, by a kind of initiatory confinement, manage to clear the decks both inside and around themselves. Bacon succeeded better than anyone in creating this exceptional, vanityless form of a singularity outside the very field of painting. He no longer projects himself into images: through images, it's himself he produces as event, without commentary. And this distinguishes him from most contemporary artists, who are all too conscious of their place in the history of art.

PP: Why don't you photograph human beings?

JB: Because only the inhuman is photogenic. It still shows through in the first photographs, even in humans, when people posed like statues, transfixed by the lens. What interests me is this cry of the object at evening in the depths of the darkroom. In its specificity [*idiotie*], every object – light or matter – comes to you as a surprise; it's no longer a matter of imposing a vision or a style. And the technique may be refined (with me, it isn't), but in the end it's always the subject who vanishes behind his lens. But this can be transposed elsewhere. Perhaps the species, by inventing a multiplicity of virtual connections, is finding a way of losing itself in the immensity of the networks. In the technical universe, the real actor is not the one you think he is. The rules of the game are doubtless not what you think they are either.

PP: Why are there fields in which you can anticipate the revenge of forms – writing and photography, for example? And why is politics not one of them?

JB: The political, strictly political, alternative has no future. It was a utopia, or a promise, arising out of industrial modernity and a purposive rationality. Neither that purpose nor that promise exists any longer. Rather, we inhabit the antagonistic dream of a violent solution, not unlike the invasion of the mirror peoples Borges wrote of.[7] The dream of all those who are condemned by the victorious emperor to be shut away behind the mirror, whence they merely reflect the image of their conquerors. They're already beginning not really to resemble those conquerors any longer; they're starting to reflect a distorted image, and one day they'll pass through the mirror again in the opposite direction; they'll resume the war, and on that occasion, writes Borges, they will not be defeated.

It's at the cost of a fantastic exclusion, a 'perfect crime', that the world is consolidating itself and homogenizing; it's the victory of the emperor monopolizing everything in his image. Metaphorically, it's the idea that all that remains on our side is a world that's material, visible, identifiable, perfectly identified. Yet somewhere else (behind the mirror) there's a kind of infinite, unidentified dark matter which could one day, one imagines, be our destiny. At any rate, from today on, it is the limit of our understanding of our material world. We run up against this total enigma of an antimatter which haunts the material world, but at the same time gives it its coherence. The world has taken shape only because this breaking of symmetry occurred, which has definitively unsettled it. Just as, elsewhere, there is the uncanny nature of the feminine, the ironic secret of the community as Hegel saw it, and the one which gives it form. There will be no end to this world because there will always be something of this radical otherness lying in wait for us. But it's no longer an active, political, rational negativity, grappling with history. It's the imminence of a revenge, of a resurrection of all that has been exiled to the other side of the mirror and held captive in the servile representation of the world of the victors, the revenge of all who have landed up on the wrong side of the universal. This power – of which we are all a part, even without knowing it – squints out from the other side of the mirror, and its ghost haunts the realized world. The more the world becomes realized, the more active is this radical illusion. This is what I termed the transparence of evil.

Chapter 7
The Childhood of Art

Philippe Petit: 'Art does not die because there isn't any any more, it dies because there is too much,' you declared in *Le Monde* of 10 June 1996. This announcement of the death of art goes back, in your view, to Marcel Duchamp. Why is he a reference for you? In what way is Duchamp the prophet of the end of art? Can you be more specific about this idea of the aesthetic principle being brought to an end?

Jean Baudrillard: It was Warhol who attracted me first. Duchamp only came afterwards. It seemed to me that with them there was a kind of anthropological fracture in the history of art, an end to the aesthetic principle. Once again, this isn't an extinction of art, but an aesthetic saturation. With Duchamp banality becomes art, and art henceforth, instead of inventing another scene, a scene of illusion, a strong scene, is content to lay hold of reality. The problem (and this is why there's a misunderstanding with the art and art-history professionals) isn't one of seeking out a specific alternative in the field of art. The theme of art is a local problematic. My objection to the guardians of contemporary art would be that they represent a self-referential, highly narcissistic milieu, and claim an imperishable status. Now, art, like reality, is a concept which has been constructed and can, therefore, be deconstructed. The end doesn't mean there's nothing any more. The problem, there as elsewhere, is what comes after the end. The question is what type of trans-aesthetic objects can come after this rupture introduced by Duchamp, without falling back into nostalgia for the lost object of painting.

PP: Arthur Danto comes close to your way of thinking on this. In *After the End of Art*,[8] he argues that we are looking into the future without any narrative of the present. We are living through the aftermath of a narrative which has reached its end and, though the memory of that narrative still colours our present consciousness, the way art became plural after the 'Brillo Box' shows up ever more clearly how the master narrative of Western art has lost its hold, and nothing has replaced it. In Danto's view, there is nothing which can replace it. What do you think of this?

JB: It's more or less the same problem for the history of art as it is for history in general. There's art in all periods, but they don't all live under the sway of the concept of history. That concept has created a continuity which has itself engendered the idea of evolution and accumulation. We claim today to be the richest era culturally; we sit astride twenty centuries of the *musée imaginaire*. There's a mystificatory, *trompe-l'œil* effect in the history of art itself, which endows itself with a dimension, an origin, an end; whereas art can't have any of these things. Art doesn't belong to the history of art. When Bacon paints his pictures, he's free of the world, he's free of any reference, and he doesn't know why he paints them. He doesn't think his art merits commentary: he does it in the raw; all that exists is the obsession with illusion, with giving form to illusion.

There's no special aesthetic status, no privilege of art – not even a negative one. I mean that if art were alone in suffering this fate of the decline of standards, this ironic and baneful fate of worthlessness, that would be a privilege and an honour still. But everything – the political, moral and philosophical spheres – is heading towards the lowest common denominator of worthlessness. This unhappy equivalence ought to be a consolation, but in fact it adds to art's own insignificance the fact of not even being alone in being insignificant – and the fact that it has, therefore, neither a privileged essence nor a privileged position. This precisely it denies, boasting a panegyrical history, reconstructed entirely to show it in a good light (as though all past cultures had worked for the greater glory of art), and some contemporary exceptions, which precisely flout the norm of art and aesthetics, to assert an incomparable predestination for itself.

Is art worthless or not? It's too worthless to be really superficial and too superficial to be really worthless.

PP: Do you like Bacon?

JB: Yes, I regret all the hullabaloo there is around him at the moment. In his interviews, Bacon spoke about sensations, technique, craft; he didn't comment on his paintings.

PP: And Deleuze's commentary on him? What do you think of that?

JB: It's a piece of Deleuze. Bacon himself said he didn't recognize himself in it. I prefer Bacon's singularity. I'd rather keep him as a pure event. All this cultural adulation surrounding him – like that around Van Gogh – all this agitation, functions as a form of control and prohibition; you even feel it physically in the exhibitions where the mass-cultural impact prevents you from looking. Not so much the mass of the public – a phenomenon which in itself evokes pathos – but the fact that art itself massifies, crosses the critical mass threshold beyond which it no longer comes under the aesthetic principle.

PP: You're a bit like the narrator of Nathalie Sarraute's *Golden Fruits*. You can't set aside the conversations and fragments of exchanges that characterize the cultural snobs who frequent exhibitions. . . .

JB: Cultural snobs are legion, but there's general collusion in this. The culture effect is refracted into all the molecules of the social body. The culture medium is totally diluted. The fact is that one can no longer dissociate art from discourse and commentary today. The artists need it. Either they go and get it from elsewhere, or they cobble it together themselves. Having once become cut off from a living principle of illusion, art has gradually become an idea. And it's around this idea of art – of an art doomed to ideas or condemned to past forms, but forms which imperceptibly become ideas – around this immortal reference of art as idea, that a gigantic collective conspiracy has hatched, a mass-aesthetic simulation which I've termed, for simplicity's sake, the art conspiracy. And I really believe this. In current art (and I'm not speaking solely of the art market, but of aesthetic values) I believe there's a shameful collusion, a collusion of the order of 'insider trading'. You might wonder how all this continues to exist, but it's like all conspiracies which, in general, serve no purpose. It's like the secret services; they're completely ineffective, but the mythology of the secret service goes merrily on. So, the fantasy of art is perpetuated by general collusion. But, once again, this isn't just the case with art: it's the same with history and the political scene – the mystery isn't their disappearance but their survival.

PP: Doesn't this amount to saying it's no longer possible to give in to regression, to the rawness of colours and forms? At the end of his life, D.H. Lawrence reflected on what a solar culture might be. I think of him because your condemnation of the cultural brings him to mind. The cultural closes off regressive processes which, as everyone knows, can turn into something progressive. It's increasingly difficult to have access to what you call the pure event, the innocence of the gaze, the nudity Gombrowicz spoke of. My instincts are bought off by the cultural.

JB: The cultural is of the order of a technology. The cultural isn't simply museums and ministries, it's a perceptual apparatus and a mental technique. We've lost sight of the idea that, basically, painting imposed itself as a system of perception. Art is an artefact and, like every artefact, it has to be able to be challenged – not so as to get back to a nature, but in the name of an illusion more powerful than its own. Ultimately, the existence of all this cultural hotchpotch is a mystery in itself. It all gives the impression that it may (and must) disappear at a stroke. The regression you speak of would be the possibility of returning to a form of primitive wildness which would sweep away this superstructure in order at last to be able to ask oneself what it means to make artificial objects appear and disappear. Art has lost this notion that it's an artifice; it has naturalized itself in the modern age on the basis of the Rousseauist idea that there's a natural foundation to man, and that you have only to strip away the social illusion to recover it. Today this has become the idea that there's a natural creativity of man which merely has to be reawakened. Everyone is capable of creating; we are all creators. This is both a Rousseauist and a naturalistic idea. Even our reality principle is based on this . . . on the idea that the world has an objective foundation, and all that's needed to find it is to strip away the illusion. Science itself partakes of this naturalistic objectivity (at least, traditional science does).

PP: As regards the naturalization of art you were speaking of, Danto writes something similar when he says that Joseph Beuys's assertion that everyone was an artist was a corollary of (or pendant to) Warhol's generalized egalitarianism. You might almost see the history of modern art as an exemplification of the history of modern individuals: 'just as the history of the traditional, figurative art of the West ha[s] been an exemplification of the assertion that human undertakings can accomplish real progress'.

Do you agree with the parallel drawn here?

JB: Yes. There's a kind of idealistic and egalitarist morality of creativity, which is of a piece with the morality of interactivity and political democracy, the idea that everyone ultimately has the same capacities for judgement as anyone else. And indeed, this is sanctioned by a legal provision: each person may legally exercise his freedom. But there's no legal jurisdiction in matters of the imagination. What would it mean for forms and their invention to be sanctioned by an individual legality? I don't think the subject as such is responsible for forms; he's responsible only for values. And here, in our general concept of art and culture, there's a massive confusion between forms and values. The extension of democracy, of its legal and egalitarian principle, to the universe of forms seems comical to me. The same tragic effect can be seen everywhere. It's in so far as sex becomes a value that it can be democratized, liberalized, moralized. But it then loses the entire secret of seduction, which is a form, a dual game with its own rules, which are not at all democratic.

PP: Could the principle of the equality of conditions be said to be the origin of this?

JB: In this egalitarian perspective, any object has the same right to be in the gallery or museum. They're all there, it's absolute democracy, the transfiguration of banality. In a way, Warhol does the same thing; he universalizes creation – which is a way of saying there are no more creators. Naturally, the idea that everyone is a creator automatically breeds indifference. Warhol deliberately plays, in an aggressive sweep, on that indifference, and says: I'm a machine. Creativity, by its very democratization, becomes mechanic. A radical desacralization: this is the same move Duchamp makes.

But then, what is there beyond this end, beyond these twists and turns? Perhaps a universe of fetish objects, as Roger Caillois sensed. That is to say, of objects which, like the fetish, have no reference, no meaning, no cultural value properly so-called. Objects this side of, or beyond, aesthetics. You can imagine a systematic profusion of ritual, fetishistic, magical objects – of the order of the universal gadget (why not?) or, alternatively, purely technical, electronic or multimedia craft productions, the total counterfeiting of the world in its virtual reality – itself an immense gadget which will put an end to the image, not just as representation but as alternative illusion. Everything produced today is perhaps ultimately just this: kinds of objects fetishized in their transparency and insignificance, without value judgements, without references and without history; objects substitutable one for another, as are most artworks today, in a kind of generality and globalization of inspiration which produces a universal radiance of culture of maximum extension and zero value. But when Warhol practises this kind of universal promotion of art, it's with a fierce irony and on the basis of an irrevocable liquidation that is quite different from the cultural democracy currently on the agenda. Duchamp and Warhol were the two great instigators of radical liquidation. But everything that was liqui-dated revives today in a museified space.

PP: All the same, there are art anarchists who escape this banalization . . . Pollock, for example.

JB: Yes, Pollock, and Hopper in particular: 'I'm not painting a story, I'm painting the light on this wall.' The idea of abstraction, too, was a crucial event. The kind of abstraction which deconstructs the object, reduces it to its simple elements, its geometrality, is in the mainstream of modernity. The paradox of abstraction – and hence of the avant-garde of modern art – is that, in believing it was 'freeing' the object from the constraints of figuration, to deliver it up to the pure play of form, it shackled it to the idea of a hidden structure, of a more rigorous, more radical objectivity than that of resemblance. That – ultra-rationalist – abstraction sought to push aside the mask of resemblance to attain to the analytic truth of the object.

Moreover, the whole aesthetic and political thrust of modernity has been towards this analytic truth. Now, what is at stake is precisely the opposite: you have to see through the identity to bring out the mask. You have to see through the truth to bring out the illusion and the secret otherness.

And the more subtle game is the one which takes reality for a mask, sees resem-blance as a trap, and plays on illusion through this very resemblance, by making it more meticulous, more obvious, heightening resemblance till it's too good to be true. This is the secret of *trompe-l'œil* and, more generally, of a figuration beyond representation and beyond its illusory surpassing in abstraction, where modern art peters out.

So, abstraction is the final phase of experimentation, which lasted as long as there were forms and values to deconstruct. But, after the end, there's a beyond. Beyond this deconstruction of the world, all kinds of compromises, all sorts of more or less agonizing revisions, of reconciliations, come in. Everything that's re-emerging today under the emblem of the postmodern has been there since the 1920s, on the basis of a definitive fulfilment – that is to say, on the basis of fully realized abstraction. A reorientation which brings the return, in no particular order – and now with no aesthetic necessity – of all the deconstructed forms and figures. Restoration, rehabilitation, repentance – recurrences and recyclings. All that had disappeared reappears. But it no longer has the same meaning, and it no longer has anything to do with aesthetic adventure. We're in the order of a fetishism without end, because that end is behind us. After the progressive movement of modernity, we have the recessive movement. After the analytic and dynamic movement, the ironic, posthumous movement. It is, in Hegel's words, 'the life, moving within itself, of that which is already dead'. But all this still presents itself as art, of which the galleries and all the parallel institutions are the funeral home.

Art itself, in its drive to invent a scene other than the real, has nothing whatever to do with an analytic truth. As soon as it has anything to do with that, it becomes the mirror of that dispersed, random reality, the reflection of waste and banality. In the exhibition on the formless at Beaubourg, we were given running paint and waste materials, but all around, and anywhere else, you see formlessness done a hundred times better and much more spectacularly than in these objects presented as emblems. These gallery objects are merely relics of a present world which has been lent an artificial aura. The formless is everywhere – except, perhaps, in this operation with, first, its formless objects, then its exhibition organizers who present the formless to us in a formal way, and, last of all, a conference where the professionals come and explain to the public how things stand with formlessness, itself a highly formal situation in which the public ends up being completely misinformed. At least three levels, then, from which the whole edifice of culture can be read off. The Beaubourg cleaners' strike was of the same order. With that strike, the Centre, an emblem of culture, was transformed into waste, whereas inside, within the framework of an exhibition on waste, it was the rubbish which was becoming culture.

PP: I would like us to talk a bit about cinema. When the events around the centenary were on, Godard declared that that commemoration 'was memorizing the honours instead of honouring the memory'. That was an ironic comment on the commemorations, but it didn't tell us how cinema, which Bazin called a popular art form and Gilles Deleuze a fully fledged form of thought, had developed today; it didn't tell us what the 'movement-image' could be a hundred years after its emergence.[9] What's your point of view on this subject? How do you see the future of cinema?

JB: Here again, the trend – towards a loss of cinematic magic – seems irreversible. It's clear that cinema has merely been on a progression towards more realism, which will continue on into computer-generated images, but was already present in the introduction of colour, of 3-D, and in high-tech cinema which has also, for its part, largely made off with the reality, or hyperreality, of the world, and managed to draw out the whole range of special effects from it. There are exceptions, such as Warhol, Altman, Godard and Antonioni: people who have managed to retrace through the image the insignificance of the world – that is to say, ultimately, its innocence – and to contribute to that insignificance with their images.

PP: Would you go so far as to say that cinema was simply a parenthesis?

JB: It seems to me that cinema has fallen into a kind of resentment of its own culture and its own history, lapsed into a performance game bordering on derision. It no longer believes in itself, though it has infinite technical and aesthetic possibilities available to it – perhaps, indeed, for that very reason. All these films burdened down with special effects can be seen, rather, as the fantasy of the machine itself, a bachelor machine with multiple layers of technicity. The promise of cinema you were speaking of is no longer what it was. It was perhaps a promise made not to be fulfilled, or to be fulfilled beyond our hopes. In fact, all the promises of modernity are of the same order: they have been accomplished technically, and, like ghosts or extras, we haunt a world which can do barely anything else now but keep its technical machinery churning.

PP: You despair, then, of recovering the lost cinematic illusion? You wrote in

Krisis of November 1996: 'Everything seems programmed to disillusion the spectator, who is left with no other conclusion than that this excess of cinema puts an end to any cinematic illusion.'

JB: Most current films, through the bloody drift of their content, the weakness of their plots and their technological tricksiness, in fact reveal an extraordinary contempt on the part of film-makers for their own tools and their own trade, a supreme contempt for the image itself, which is prostituted to any special effect whatsoever; and, consequently, contempt for the viewer, who is called upon to figure as impotent voyeur of this prostitution of images, this promiscuity of all forms behind the alibi of violence. There is in fact no real violence in this, nothing of a theatre of cruelty, merely a second-level irony, the knowing wink of quotation, which is no longer of the order of cinematic culture, but derives from the resentment culture feels towards itself, that culture which precisely cannot manage to come to an end, and is becoming infinitely debased – debasement being raised to the power of an aesthetic and spiritual commodity, bitter and obsolescent, which we consume as a 'work of art' with the same sly complicity with which we savour the debasement of the political class. The sabotaging of the image by the image professionals here joins the sabotaging of the political by the politicians themselves.

Unimpeded View
or The Definitive Uncertainty
of Thought

That which in the object is irreducible to the subject.

That which in the subject is irreducible to itself, to the concepts and formulas which analyse it, and by which it analyses itself.

That which in exchange is irreducible to the law of equivalence.

That which in the social is irreducible to the social itself (the accursed share, the critical mass).

That which in history is irreducible to history: the event.

That which in sexuality is irreducible to sex: seduction.

Going through all the disciplines to arrive at the enigma of their object. Using them in a transversal, allusive, metaphorical, elliptical, ironic mode – not realist, not objective, not methodical, not referential. Isn't analysis itself a parody of its object? But the latter isn't merely the blind substratum of the interpretation either. The thing that could be got rid of once it had yielded up its meaning. Something in it mocks us and our analyses.

What, then, is the obsession, the secret motive, the endless finality underlying this progression? Finding the irreducible point which gives an unimpeded view of the world.

The trend in all disciplines is to see their objects disappearing. There is no more a truth of anthropology than there is of primitive societies, but in their place the current revolution of our whole social logic, through the imagination of the savage, the radical otherness of which far outstrips the realist logic of the human sciences. The veracity of the social sphere is that of the crucial point at which it becomes an exponential phenomenon, at which it reaches the critical point of non-return, when it disappears into the masses or, by contrast, blazes in a symbolic incandescence and a challenge to its own values. Such is also the veracity of analysis. At any rate, when sociology finally gets around to stating some coherent propositions about the social, society will long ago have disappeared. It is already disappearing. Only sociological metalanguage preserves the fossilized traces of it.

The human will itself is becoming translucent. Each of our actions is at the same erratic stage as the microscopic particle; we cannot evaluate both its ends and its means. You cannot calculate both the price of a human life and its statistical value. Just as we cannot simultaneously calculate the velocity and the position of a particle, so we are unable to evaluate both the real event and its shifting meaning in information; nor, in a particular complex process, can we tell cause from effect; nor, in the Stockholm syndrome, tell the terrorist from the hostage; nor, in their mortal symbiosis, the virus from the cell – any more than one can tell subject from object in subatomic physics experiments.

Now, if we cannot grasp both the genesis and the singularity of the event, the appearance of things and their meaning, then one of two things is possible: either we master the meaning, and the appearances escape us; or the meaning escapes us, and appearances are preserved. By the very play of this uncertainty, things are moving further and further from their meaning, and doubtless even from each other – the world here accentuating its flight into strangeness and emptiness.

Meteorological stage of the economic, the political, the social, the aesthetic. Meteorological sign of uncertainty.

Cosmopolitan stage, immediately international, of the only events possible.

Viral, fractal stage of the insolidity of all things, which scatter into a secretly de-polarized space. Nothing has the function of signifying any more. Everything's just there to fill up the empty space of language, which has become the random site of all promiscuities, the site of the non-discrimination and obscenity of the formula. Nothing confronts anything else any more – and this includes ideas. All things release their repellent forces. The chain reaction stage, of which atomic energy remains the prototype. Nuclear abreaction, including the abreaction of information, transfers all processes into a dimension incommensurate with history. Liberation everywhere triggers off exponential processes, entirely different from symbolic equilibria. All functions cease to be comparative or superlative and become exponential, exceeding their ends and their compass. They enter an interminable phase – uncontrolled growth or persistent vegetative state. Liberation everywhere brings with it a fusion, then a superfusion of energies.

In this advance towards extreme phenomena, the utopias linked to the different disciplines collapse (for each secretes a method and a utopia). No more political subversion, no more 'liberation' of desire or the unconscious, nor hypostasis of the signifier, nor even the utopian leitmotiv of alienation accompanied by a radical subjectivity. The end of metalanguage, the end of metaphysics, the end of metaphor, all giving way to the pure sign, the pure event. For everything is achieved, there is nothing to be found at the end any more; everything is already here – that is to say, beyond the end.

The only fatal strategy: find the blind, tangential, potential point that is irreducible, the reversion point of all these systems. And for this, the analysis itself has to become object, to become a material object, a material event of language – and become so ironically. Retaining the effect of silence, of ruse, of irreducible non-meaning which is that of the object. Taking into account objective irony, which is that of the world, never its own.

It is no longer the human which thinks the world. Today, it is the inhuman which thinks us. And not at all metaphorically, but by a kind of viral homology, by the direct infiltration of a viral, contaminative, virtual, inhuman thought. We are the fetish objects of a thought that is no longer ours, or that is its uncontrollable outgrowth. We can now grasp what we are only from an omega point external to the human, on the basis of objects far more distant, far stranger than those of our sciences, which are bearers of a radical uncertainty and on which we can no longer at all impose our perspectives, on the basis of objects which have become for us strange attractors. . . . A perspective that is, all in all, heroic – thought choosing the path of renunciation rather than abolishing its concept by realizing it. A criminal thought which, speaking evil, illusion, seduction, duplicity and the irreconcilable character of the forces which divide up the 'real' world between themselves, is opposed as such to that perfect crime that is the enterprise of the unconditional reconciliation of the world. A thinking that is no stranger to imposture – like truth, which, as we know, is eternally veiled, and is thus itself an eternal imposture.

'We must not believe that the truth remains the truth when we strip it of its veil' – thus, truth has no naked existence.

We must not believe that the real remains the real when its illusion has been dispelled – thus, the real has no objective reality.

Notes

Part One

1.   '*La pensée unique*' has in recent years been one of the watchwords of French political discussion. It implies a single-track thinking of the kind once referred to in Britain by the acronym TINA ('There is no alternative'). The editor of *Le Monde diplomatique* defined it as 'the translation into ideological terms, with universalist pretensions, of the interests of a set of economic forces, in particular those of international capital', and identified its major sources as the great economic and monetary institutions: the World Bank, the IMF, the OECD, GATT, the European Commission, etc. (Ignacio Ramonet, 'La pensée unique', *Le Monde diplomatique*, 490, January 1995, p. 1). [*Trans.*]

2.   Gilles Deleuze, *Cinéma 2: L'Image-temps*, Paris: Minuit, 1985.

3.   Jean Baudrillard, *The Transparency of Evil*, trans. James Benedict, London: Verso, 1993, p. 85 (translation modified).

4.   Alain Besançon, *The Falsification of the Good: Soloviev and Orwell*, trans. Matthew Screech, Concord, MA: Paul & Co., 1994.

5.   The term 'transparence du mal' and the related terminology still seem to generate considerable confusion. I have recently even seen the term 'transparaître'

117

translated as 'transpire', which is distinctly troubling, since 'transparaître' is simply used by Baudrillard in its everyday meaning of 'to show through' (Robert: 'se montrer au travers de quelque chose'; an obsolete English equivalent, 'transpare', seems to have died out in the seventeenth century). Although the introduction of unrelated notions of 'transpiration' is not especially misleading in the context, it unnecessarily introduces an entirely different metaphor.

The problems undoubtedly originate, as Baudrillard himself has admitted in one public interview, in his use of the noun 'transparence' to render what would perhaps more usually be termed 'transparition'. Andrew Wernick, in an excellent review of *The Transparency of Evil* (in the Internet journal *CTheory* [www.ctheory.com/ctheory.html]) speaks of this as the 'impossible term "transparition"', but it should be noted that the term is 'impossible' only in English – at least in the sense that it does not figure in the *OED*.

My own solution to this thorny problem has been to enlist the unusual English variant 'transparence'. This word, though somewhat odd, does have the virtue of having been used in the past in English in the sense intended (e.g. 'Motive may be detected through the transparence of tendency', R.W. Hamilton, *Popular Education*, second edition, London 1845). [*Trans.*]

6. Roger Garaudy, *Les mythes fondateurs de la politique israélienne*, Paris: La Vieille Taupe, 1995. On 27 February 1998, Garaudy was fined 24,000 francs for publishing this work. [*Trans.*]

7. François Laruelle, *Une biographie de l'homme ordinaire*, Paris: Aubier, 1985.

8. E.M. Cioran, *Histoire et utopie*, Paris: Gallimard, 1987.

9. The reference is to the investigation of the dealings of Jean Tiberi, the Gaullist mayor of Paris, and particularly to the circumstances in which his son acquired the tenancy of a flat in the rue Censier. On the details of this 'affair' and its apparent judicial 'burying' when Jacques Toubon became Garde des Sceaux, see *Libération* of 20 June 1996, first edition (headline 'Abracadabra, l'affaire Tiberi n'est plus là'). [*Trans.*]

10. Jean Baudrillard, *The Consumer Society*, trans. Chris Turner, London: Sage,

1998. This work was, in fact, originally published in French in 1969, but the revised edition on which the translation is based appeared in 1970. [*Trans.*]

11. Yves Michaud, *La violence apprivoisée*, Paris: Hachette, 1996.

12. Alain Brossat, *Fêtes sauvages de la démocratie*, Paris: Austral, 1996.

13. Florence Rey was the young woman who, having until that point been a quiet and unremarkable school student, suddenly – and, as it seemed, quite inexplicably – embarked on a murderous jaunt across Paris. [*Trans.*]

14. Jean Baudrillard, *The Perfect Crime*, trans. Chris Turner, London: Verso, 1996.

15. 'Les Mercredis de l'histoire' is the weekly political documentary slot of the Franco–German TV channel Arte. The reference here is almost certainly to Luc de Heusch's film 'Une République devenue folle: Rwanda, 1894–1994', broadcast on 12 June 1996. [*Trans.*]

16. See Note 1 above.

17. Baudrillard has made repeated references to the 'memory of water' affair in recent years. See, for example, *The Illusion of the End*, trans. Chris Turner, Cambridge: Polity, 1994, pp. 30–31. [*Trans.*]

Part Two

1. Jean Baudrillard, *America*, trans. Chris Turner, London: Verso, 1988, p. 6.

2. Ibid., p. 89.

3. Jorge Luis Borges, 'Fauna of Mirrors', in *The Book of Imaginary Beings*, Harmondsworth: Penguin, 1974, pp. 67–8.

4. *America*, p. 28.

5. See Maurice Blanchot, *The Space of Literature*, trans. Ann Smock, Lincoln, NE: University of Nebraska Press, 1982, p. 257.

6. Susan Sontag, *On Photography*, London: Allen Lane, 1978, p. 179.

7. See above, Note 3.

8. Arthur C. Danto, *After the End of Art: Contemporary Art and the Pale of*

History (A.W. Mellon Lectures in the Fine Arts, 1995), Princeton, NJ: Princeton University Press, 1997.

9. See Gilles Deleuze, *Cinema 1: Movement-Image*, trans. Hugh Tomlinson and Barbara Habberjam, Minneapolis, MN: University of Minnesota Press, 1986.

Printed in the United States
by Baker & Taylor Publisher Services